Complete
Beading

FOR BEGINNERS

KAREN REMPEL

HARBOUR PUBLISHING

Pages 13-26 • Stringing beads to make necklaces, bracelets and other beadwork.

Multiple strand necklace
(below) with Italian oxblood coral beads, Turkish coin silver beads and clasp.
Karen Glesby, Silver Moon.

Necklace and pendant
(left) strung with antique chevrons and Peking glass, with antique Guatemalan coin silver pendant.
Karen Glesby, Silver Moon

Multiple strand bracelet
(right) with lapis lazuli beads and antique coin silver beads and clasp.
Karen Glesby, Silver Moon.

Necklace and bracelet
(above) with antique glass trade beads, lapis lazuli, cobalt blue dogons, African padres, millefiori and Peking glass trade beads, chevrons, coin silver beads and clasp.
Karen Glesby, Silver Moon.

Beaded eye catcher
(below) strung with seed and bugle beads and semi-precious stones, fastened with plastic loops.
Josephine MacDowall.

"Treasure necklace"
strung with pendants of lapis lazuli and coin silver beads, rock crystal, semi-precious stones, antique chevron and cobalt blue trade beads and Chinese enamelled beads.
Karen Glesby, Silver Moon.

ii

2 • Earrings

Pages 27-42 • *Creating earrings using materials you can find in bead stores.*

Earrings (below) made from Chinese carved turquoise and gold-plated coin silver beads. *Karen Glesby, Silver Moon.*

Double hoop earrings (above) strung with glass, ceramic and metallic beads using findings available in most bead shops. *Kerri Luciani.*

Abstract earrings (above) made by hand-twisting wire and stringing with purple wooden beads. *Kerri Luciani.*

Sun and moon earrings. (below) *Kerri Luciani.*

Earrings (below) strung with black onyx and Chinese gold-plated coin silver beads. *Karen Glesby, Silver Moon.*

Earrings (above) made with antique Tibetan turquoise, Chinese coral, Balouchi pendant and Ottoman coins. *Karen Glesby, Silver Moon.*

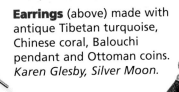

Dangle earrings (right) with hand-carved lapis lazuli and coin silver beads. *Karen Glesby, Silver Moon.*

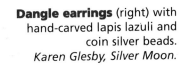

3•Off-Loom Weaving

Pages 43-66 • Weaving beads together with thread to create all kinds of beadwork.

Cat Purse
(right) with crocheted knit top; the remainder of the bag was created using the *peyote stitch. Helen Rogers.*

Necklace
with *peyote stitch* strap and pendant, accented with carved amber and ivory nut beads.
Lene Giershoj Baldry.

"Lace collar"
made from synthetic pearl seed beads, and created using the *netting* technique.
From a private collection.

Collar-net necklace
woven using *netting*, with copper bugle beads and glass seed and pony beads. See page 47 for project instructions. *Jacqui Bellfontaine.*

Beaded pipe bag (left) made with Czechoslovakian Charlotte beads using flat and round *peyote stitch* and oval mandala stitch. With deerskin, silver and citrine. *John Binzley.*

iv

4 • Loom Weaving

Pages 67-80 • Creating a beaded "fabric" using a bead loom.

Belt (left) made with a strip of loom woven seed beads and backed with leather. *From a private collection.*

Leather purse (above) with loom woven butterfly motif and looped end fringes. *Lene Giershoj Baldry.*

Snake (left) with loom woven body and tail. The head was constructed using the *peyote stitch,* an off-loom weaving technique. *Lene Giershoj Baldry.*

Loom woven medicine bag (below) lined with silk and inset with rhodochrosite cabochon. Fringe contains three quartz points and rhodochrosite chips. *Barbara Volk.*

Loom woven barrette (above) with side fringes. Backed with leather and glued to barrette base. *Jacqui Bellefontaine.*

Pages 81-98 • Using beads to decorate clothes, cushions, scarves and purses.

Dress (right) features a lace sheath embroidered with pearl and crystal seed beads. Seed bead fringes highlight the skirt. *From a private collection.*

Phoenix design leather purse (left) in applied beading using both straight and *contour* stitches. Hand-laced and fully lined with leather. Two silver conchos are inlaid with turquoise. *Wendy Ellsworth.*

circa 1840 Red River Métis Capote (left) quilled and painted on buckskin. Felt top hat with quilled hat band and ostrich feather. *Angela Swedberg.*

Cotton festival blouse (above) with beadwork and embroidery. From the Puebla region of Mexico. *From the collection of the Center for the Study of Beadwork.*

Tsuu T'ina gauntlet, (right) made of unsmoked buckskin, decorated with seed beads, date unknown. *Courtesy of the Glenbow Museum.*

6•Other Things

Pages 99-109 • Other things you can make with beads, such as barrettes, dream catchers, rings and pins.

...och (right) made with seed ...ads and cabochons backed ...leather. The dangles and ...ed fringe are strung with ...gle beads and small stone and metal beads. *Kerri Luciani.*

...oth brooches (below) are ...reated from a combination of *appliqué* and off-loom ...veaving techniques. ...he cabochon and ...netal button are ...lued onto a stiff ...eather backing. *...erri Luciani.*

Dream catcher earrings (right) with lapis lazuli beads and gold-plated feathers. *Jacqui Bellefontaine.*

Rings (left) created using different bead weaving techniques. From left to right: loom weaving, *square* stitch, *netting*, *chevron* stitch and *daisy chain*. *Karen Rempel.*

Beaded barrettes (right) feature bases that are wrapped with wire strung with glass and metal beads. *Kerri Luciani and Jill Diebel.*

Pages 110-117 • Making your own beads out of paper and polymer clay.

Necklace and pendant
(right) made with hand-made polymer clay beads with metal spacer beads.
Jill Diebel.

Heart and star brooches
(right) are created by fusing together and flattening polymer clay beads. The pin finding is glued onto the back.
Jill Diebel.

Earrings (above) with hand-made polymer clay beads, wood and metal beads and bells.
Jill Diebel.

Necklace (above) strung with metal spacer beads and hand-made paper beads painted black and green to create uniform colours.
Micheline Larose and Georges Gamache.

Hand-made paper beads
(right) in assorted sizes and shapes.
Micheline Larose and Georges Gamache.

Complete
Beading for
Beginners

Complete Beading for Beginners

Karen Rempel

HARBOUR PUBLISHING

HARBOUR PUBLISHING CO. LTD.
P.O. Box 219
Madeira Park, BC Canada V0N 2H0

Cover and colour photo section designed by Roger Handling.
Interior designed by Mary White.
Colour photos and project photos by Lionel Trudel, unless otherwise stated.
Chapter head photos by Joel Johnstone.
Line drawings and diagrams by Gaye Hammond.
Beadwork by the following artists:

Lene Giershoj Baldry, Langley, BC. Loom woven lizard, cover right, title page; Peyote stitch necklace and pendant, iv; Leather purse with butterfly motif, v; Snake, v.

Jacqui Bellfontaine, Quadra Island, BC. Dream catcher earrings, cover left, vii, 99; Collar-net necklace, iv, 47; Loom woven barrette, v; Fringed earrings, 27 right, 30; Beader, bead embroidery sampler, 82.

John Binzley, Jerome, Arizona and Bali. Beaded pipe bag, iv. Photograph © Alice Scherer, Center for the Study of Beadwork.

Center for the Study of Beadwork, Portland, Oregon. Cotton festival blouse, vi. Photograph © Alice Scherer, Center for the Study of Beadwork.

Copper Coyote Beads, Ltd. Tucson, Arizona. Beading graph paper, 118, 122; 9430 E. Golf Link #286, Tucson, AZ 85730 USA

Jill Diebel, Gibsons, BC. Barrettes, vii; Earrings, viii; Heart and star brooches, viii; Polymer clay necklace and pendant, viii.

Wendy Ellsworth, Quakertown, Pennsylvania. Mask Purse, cover bottom left; Phoenix design leather purse, vi. Photographs © Alice Scherer, Center for the Study of Beadwork.

Glenbow Museum, Calgary, Alberta. Ojibwa shoulder bag detail, cover top left; Tsuu T'ina gauntlet, page vi; courtesy of the Glenbow Museum.

Karen Glesby, Silver Moon Trading Co. Ltd., Vancouver, BC. Lapis lazuli dangle earrings, cover left, iii; Necklace and bracelet, cover middle, ii; Coral multiple strand necklace, ii; Multiple strand bracelet, ii; Necklace and pendant, ii; Treasure necklace, ii; Chinese turquoise earrings, iii; Onyx earrings, iii; Tibetan turquoise earrings, iii.

Micheline Larose and Georges Gamache, Gibsons, BC. Assorted paper beads, viii; Paper bead necklace, viii.

Kerri Luciani, Gibsons, BC. Fringed earring, cover right; Polymer clay beads, cover top right, back cover; Abstract earrings, iii; Double hoop earrings, iii; Sun and moon earrings, iii; Barrettes, vii; Seed bead and cabochon brooches, vii.

Josephine MacDowall, Vancouver, BC. Beaded eye catcher, ii.

Karen Rempel, Vancouver, BC. Beaded rings, vii, 99; Lace and bead choker, 14; Braided bead necklace, 16; Dangle earrings, 28; Peyote bracelet, 43, 51; Daisy chain bracelet, 44; Loom woven bracelet, 68, 118; Barrette, 81.

Helen Rogers, Davis, California. Cat purse, iv. Photograph © Alice Scherer, Center for the Study of Beadwork.

Angela Swedberg, Port Orchard, Washington. Design, bead embroidery sampler, 82; Red River Métis capote, vi. Colour photograph © Wally Hampton.

Barbara Volk, Timonium, Maryland. Loom woven medicine bag, v. Photograph © Alice Scherer, Center for the Study of Beadwork.

Donna Wasserstrom, Columbus, Ohio. *Abelam* (leather purse), cover left middle. Photograph © Alice Scherer, Center for the Study of Beadwork.

Printed and bound in Canada by Friesen Printers.

Canadian Cataloguing in Publication Data

Rempel, Karen, 1965–
  Complete beading for beginners

  Includes index.
  ISBN 1-55017-102-X

  1. Beadwork. I. Title.
TT860.R45 1995   745.58'2   C95-910836-X

For Kim, Kirsten, Kurt and Katherine Rempel.

As I wrote this book I pictured you as the readers.

Contents

Introduction

ANCIENT BEADS WERE MADE OF...

Australia—kangaroo bones

India—seashells, carnelian, stone

Africa—ostrich egg shells

Central and South America—jade, gold, snail shell

North America—shell, pearl, bone, teeth, stone

Egypt and Mesopotamia—lapis lazuli, turquoise, amethyst, gold, ivory, obsidian

Europe—coral, amber, pearls

China, Korea and Japan—jade, fossil dinosaur egg shell

Bead stores often carry ancient-looking beads made of natural or synthetic materials.

Maybe you've loved beads for as long as you can remember, as I have. Or perhaps you first noticed beads when a bead store opened nearby or you saw a friend's bead-embroidered shirt. Once you become aware of beads, you'll probably notice them everywhere: beautiful beads from all over the globe, of every colour and shape, combined in countless styles.

When I bought my first beads in the late seventies, I had to search among the model airplanes in a hobby shop. Now many stores specialize in beads and beading materials. There are bead newsletters, magazines, mail-order catalogues and societies.

People of all ages are discovering the wonder of beads. Creating a unique, decorative and functional work of art never loses its thrill. Beading does call for time, money and skill, but you have many options. You can spend five dollars or five hundred on materials. You can spend minutes on a necklace or months on a wall hanging. Even with no experience you can quickly make a gorgeous bead-and-leather pendant.

You'll also discover you can bead inexpensive gifts. You can make bead jewellery: a multicoloured strand of seed beads, ancient coin earrings (fake or real), a single bead on a leather thong, an elaborate bracelet with ethnic beads, or an elegant black velvet choker with a silver heart pendant. You can also bead picture frames, wall hangings, hatbands, bead-embroidered clothing, sculptures and lampshades. If you can think of it, chances are you can make it with beads. One bead store sells beautiful bead-and-wire spiders, and I recently met a beader who makes incredible beaded snakes and lizards.

Beads today reflect thousands of years of cultural and technological development. Archaeologists estimate that the first bead—an animal tooth on a hide thong—was created about 40,000 years ago. Beads are common finds in ancient graves, and help to reveal early trade and settlement routes.

Beads' significance changed over time. The earliest beads were talismans to gain power over food animals such as the woolly mammoth. When our ancestors formed larger groups in which it was harder to know everyone by sight, beads became a means of personal identification.

About 10,000 years ago, when we started farming, beads grew more popular. We soon used each new technology for bead-making. Beads met our changing needs: intercession with the gods, personal adornment, status symbols and creative expression.

New beaders take an interest in the craft every day. Even by admiring beads you become part of their rich history.

Welcome to the amazing, timeless world of beads. May it bring you much pleasure!

BEAD LORE

In ancient times *people scattered beads like seeds under Asian temples to ensure a good harvest.*

The Kogi people *of Columbia used beads in ritual offerings to bring luck to a family moving into a new home.*

Eight thousand years *before Europeans arrived, North American peoples were making, wearing and trading beads. Later they used beads as wampum, a form of exchange.*

The Egyptians or Mesopotamians *invented faience, a ceramic material decorated with coloured glazes, around 4000 BCE to make beads resembling precious stones such as turquoise and lapis lazuli. This was the first mass production of imitation luxury goods for the poorer classes.*

Venetian glass makers *from 1490 to 1540 CE faced the death penalty if they revealed glass bead-making secrets.*

A trader's bead sample card, *used before 1900 in trading with the Crow people, shows great demand for tiny glass seed beads; more than eighty colours were available.*

In the Philippines, *two beads are placed in a cup during wedding ceremonies to bind the partners together.*

Young Zulu women *weave beads together as love letters to their boyfriends or husbands, expressing their feelings of love, yearning or sadness at being parted. The colours and patterns signify the letter's meaning—red might mean "My eyes are red from weeping"—and form a secret language between the lovers.*

How to Use This Book

This book is arranged to help you start beading as quickly as possible.

The many beading techniques are organized into five broad categories, each with its own chapter and starter projects: *Stringing, Earrings, Off-Loom Weaving, Loom Weaving* and *Bead Embroidery*. The instructional chapters are followed by six extremely useful chapters of general information needed for all types of beading—*Other Things You Can Bead, Making Your Own Beads, Planning and Design, Solutions to Common Beading Problems, Basic Knots* and *Tools and Materials*—followed by a *Bibliography* and *Index*.

● If you want to jump right in, refer to the sidebar on the left side of this page. If you saw a bead-embroidered T-shirt, for example, and want to make one, turn to the page given for Embroidered clothing. Or choose one of the projects in *italics*.

● If you want to start beading right away but don't know what you want to make, read further. The chapter descriptions that follow explain the different kinds of beading in more detail. If one of them catches your interest, turn to the start of the chapter and read the introductory comments, which tell you even more about each kind of beading. The first five chapters also include start-up projects that introduce you to the technique on a step-by-step basis with all the information you need, from preparing a shopping list to applying professional finishing techniques. The introductory projects are followed by techniques you can use for more advanced projects. Sprinkled through the chapters you'll also find lots of working tips in the margins.

Chapter 1 / **STRINGING** / Page 13
Stringing is just what it seems: threading beads in a line. You can string a simple choker, a necklace of many strands or a complicated wall-hanging. But which threads do you use with which beads? How do you make the right knots? This chapter tells you all about it.

> **Projects:** two kinds of necklaces.

Chapter 2 / **EARRINGS** / Page 27
Earrings made of beads require an assortment of little metal parts called **findings** that connect beads to each other and to your ear. (Note: Whenever you see a term in **bold** type, you can find a complete description of the term in Chapter 11, *Tools and Materials*.) Chapter 2 describes these findings and how to use them, and how to make earrings using many techniques.

> **Projects:** two kinds of earrings.

Chapter 3 / **OFF-LOOM WEAVING** / Page 43
Off-Loom Weaving is the most common way of arranging beads in patterns to form beaded "fabric," which can be as narrow as a few beads or as wide as a curtain. Off-loom weaving is used to make all kinds of jewellery, from necklaces to rings to earrings. It is also used to cover objects, like bottles, hats or canes. The *daisy chain* is one of many off-loom weaving techniques described in this chapter. (Note: Whenever you see a term in *italic* type, it means the technique is explained elsewhere in the book. You can quickly find where by looking in the index.)

> **Projects:** two kinds of bracelets, one necklace.

Chapter 4 / **LOOM WEAVING** / Page 67
Loom Weaving is another way to make beaded fabric, by using a special beading loom. Loom weaving allows you to produce strips of colourful beaded patterns for making chokers, decorating belts and a thousand other purposes.

> **Project:** one bracelet.

Chapter 5 / **BEAD EMBROIDERY** / Page 81
Bead Embroidery is much the same as regular embroidery, only you use beads instead of coloured thread to decorate material. Bead embroidery can be used to create brilliant colour patches on jeans, leather moccasins and other personal items.

> **Project:** one bead-embroidered sampler to hang up or sew onto a jacket or T-shirt.

Chapter 6 / **OTHER THINGS YOU CAN BEAD** / Page 99
The chapter on *Other Things You Can Bead* shows how to combine

the previous chapters' techniques with new findings and materials to make rings, barrettes, brooches, wall hangings and dream catchers.

Chapter 7 / **MAKING YOUR OWN BEADS** / Page 110

Some of the most beautiful and fascinating beadwork creations are made from hand-made beads. This chapter shows how to achieve spectacular results using materials like paper and Fimo®.

Chapter 8 / **PLANNING AND DESIGN** / Page 118

When you're ready to begin creating your own beadwork designs, look at the *Planning and Design* chapter. It describes what to consider when you plan your own projects, gives you tips about preparing designs and offers ways to come up with design ideas.

Chapter 9 / **SOLUTIONS TO COMMON BEADING PROBLEMS** / Page 126

Nobody gets through a beading project without running into a few problems, especially at the start. This chapter is loaded with nifty solutions for every situation you are likely to encounter.

Chapter 10 / **BASIC KNOTS** / Page 131

Beads are the star attraction of beadwork, but knots are what hold it all together and make it last. There are many different knots for many different situations and this chapter tells you what they are.

Chapter 11 / **TOOLS AND MATERIALS** / Page 133

In some ways this is the most important chapter in the book. Not only does it provide an extensive education about the many different types of beads, beading tools and materials that make beading a unique craft, it contains a wealth of helpful hints. Of special interest to beginners are the **Tool kit** heading and basic beading materials, marked with the ✄ symbol.

BIBLIOGRAPHY / Page 149

The *Bibliography* lists many other publications that give detailed information on specific areas of beading, offer more advanced guidance or feed the dedicated beader's hunger for ever more knowledge of the craft.

INDEX / Page 153

This *Index* is no ordinary index, but a key feature that helps all the parts of the book work together. Everything you need to know about beading is explained somewhere in this book, and the index is the thing that tells you where to look. Use it often!

Margin notes like this contain working tips that give you extra information about the projects and techniques.

Key to Symbols

bold / This term is defined in Chapter 11, Tools and Materials.

italic / This technique is explained elsewhere in the book—to find out where, look it up in the index.

✄ / This basic tool or material is useful to beginners.

Chapter One
Stringing

Bead stringing is a great place for a new beader to start. You'll have the fun of combining different bead shapes and colours without worrying about complicated techniques. And that's what beading is all about: choosing from an amazing assortment of beads to find a combination that's right for you. Bead stringing rewards your efforts instantly. In minutes you can make a gorgeous necklace, choker or bracelet and wear it right away.

Stringing beads, the first method of combining beads ever invented, has remained popular through a 30,000-year evolution in beading techniques. Most people learn to string beads as children, often with big, brightly coloured plastic beads that pop together. Stringing, despite its simplicity, has produced some of the most stunning jewellery ever made.

This chapter begins with two easy—and inexpensive—bead stringing projects. The following sections discuss factors to consider when choosing stringing materials and describe additional stringing techniques. The final section provides valuable information about how to finish your strands of beads to make them functional and beautiful pieces of jewellery.

Lace and Bead Choker Project

This project shows you how to make an attractive necklace or choker by knotting a few beads in position on a leather lace. The necklace is quick and easy to make, but your end result will be professionally finished, thanks to lace-end crimps and a clasp. Once you've finished the project, you could use the same technique to create a matching bracelet. The necklace in the photograph is made of green clay beads, gold-coloured disks and green leather cord (and it cost less than five dollars to make), but you can choose any colour you like. You may also decide to use a different number of beads.

You'll find *basic materials for this project fully described in Chapter 11,* **Tools and Materials**. *Look for the ✿ symbol.*

SHOPPING LIST
- beads (make sure the holes are big enough so the cord will go through the beads)
- leather lace (1 m or 1 yard)
- 2 lace-end crimps
- 1 clasp

TOOL KIT
- needle-nose pliers
- scissors
- tape measure
- adhesive (optional)

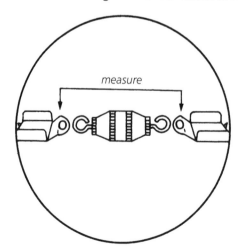

MEASURING YOUR LACE

Not sure *whether you want to make a necklace or a choker? String your beads on a thread and hold it up to your neck at a mirror. Try out different lengths. (Don't put the beads on the lace until you've decided on a stringing order, as adding and removing beads can ruin the finish on the lace.)*

Decide how long you want the necklace or choker to be. Then line up the lace-end crimps on either side of the clasp to see how much room the finishing will take. Measure from the bend in one lace-end crimp to the bend in the other. Subtract this amount from the desired length of the necklace to calculate the length of the finished cord. Write this down. Add one inch for the knots and cut the cord to this length. (You'll trim the excess later in these steps.)

measure

BEADING

1. Centre the beads on the cord. Tie an *overhand knot* in the cord on each side of the beads. Leave a tiny space between the knots and the beads so the beads hang naturally.

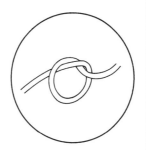

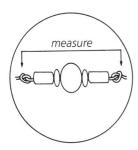

2. Measure from the outer edge of one knot to the outer edge of the other knot; subtract this length from the amount you calculated under "Measuring Your Lace."

3. Divide by two the amount you calculated in step 2. The cord on each side of the knot should be this long. Trim the cord ends to this length.

4. Position one end of the lace in a lace-end crimp. (If you wish, apply a tiny drop of adhesive to the lace inside the crimp.) Use needle-nose pliers to press one side of the crimp shut, then the other side. Do the same on the other lace-end crimp.

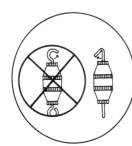

5. Attach the clasp loops to the loops of the lace-end crimps. Open the clasp loops by twisting the end of the wire to the side. (Don't pull outward to open the loop; this would cause the wire to weaken and lose its nice round shape.)

That's all there is to it. You've taken just minutes to make a beautiful new piece of jewellery, and you've learned some basic beading skills.

Do not poke a hole in the lace for the little triangular prong of the crimp to go through. When you squeeze the crimp shut with pliers the prong helps to grip the lace.

If your pliers don't have smooth jaws, wrap their tips with masking tape so they won't scratch the surface of the lace-end crimp.

Braided Bead Necklace Project

This project shows you how to make a braided three-strand necklace in three colours. It illustrates one method of using jewellery findings to finish multistrand beadwork. You'll also put your design skills to good use when you choose the beads.

Seed beads offer the simplest way to make this necklace, but you can choose any light to medium-weight beads you like. Just make sure your nylon or silk thread is strong enough to hold their weight. Try faceted glass or plastic beads, small wooden beads, lightweight clay beads or glass pony beads. Any of these can give striking results. Or mix bead types to create a textured effect.

You can experiment with colour too. The instructions call for a single colour on each strand, as shown in the photograph, but you can mix and match colours randomly or in an alternating pattern. Choose thread to match. Once you see the results, you'll probably want to try this technique with bracelets too.

SHOPPING LIST
- beads (three colours)
- nylon or silk thread
- 1 clasp
- 2 calotte crimps (also called bead tips)

TOOL KIT
- beeswax
- 3 beading needles (threader optional)
- scissors
- needle-nose pliers
- tape measure
- adhesive
- transparent or masking tape (for anchoring the beadwork while you braid)

MEASURING YOUR THREAD
You'll need to double the threads for this project if you use nylon thread. A single strand is strong enough if you use silk thread. Decide how long you want the necklace to be, add an extra 1/3 to the length, then add 20 cm (8 inches) for attaching the crimps and clasp. For example, if you

Silk thread is strong and lovely, and it stretches less than nylon thread, but nylon is more resistant to fraying and decay.

Stackable, transparent fishing tackle containers are handy for storing small beads.

want to make a necklace 45 cm long, add one third of 45 cm (15 cm, giving you 60 cm), then add 20 cm for a total thread length of 80 cm. Double the overall length if you use nylon thread. Cut three threads. Put a needle onto each thread. If you use a doubled thread, slide the needle to the centre and wax the thread to prevent tangling.

BEADING

You don't need to worry about the size of the bead holes if the needle will go through once. You can use irregularly shaped beads, too, to add interesting texture to the strand.

1. Make an *overhand knot* to tie the loose ends of all three (doubled) threads together, about 8 cm (3 inches) from their ends. (See Chapter 10, *Basic Knots*, for instructions on tying the knots used in this project.)

2. Pass all three needles through the hole in a calotte crimp and slide the crimp until it rests against the knot, with the cups of the crimp facing the knot.

3. Use one needle to pick up one colour of beads until the strand of beads is 1/3 longer than the desired length of your necklace. Be sure to press the beads firmly against the calotte crimp.

4. Tie a *slip knot* in the thread to hold the beads in place. Do not remove the needle.

5. Repeat steps 3 and 4 for the other two threads, using a different colour of beads on each.

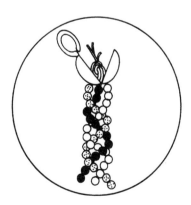

6. Arrange the three strands side by side and braid them together. Always cross the strands close to the previous crossing, making the braid as tight as possible. (Most threads stretch a little; the braid will loosen later.)

7. When you've braided as close as possible to the slip knots, measure the length of the braid. The finished length of a braid varies according to the braid's tightness and the bead size. If the braid is shorter or longer than you planned, this is the time to add or remove some beads. Untie

Beeswax can prevent long pieces of thread (required for most techniques) from tangling in knots. If you're using unwaxed thread, run the thread twice over a lump of beeswax or an ordinary candle. Then pinch the thread between your thumb and forefinger, and pull it through with your other hand; this will distribute the wax evenly along the length of the thread and remove excess wax. Beeswax also strengthens the thread, prevents fraying, makes knots more secure and protects against moisture. Remember to rewax periodically, because the wax rubs off inside the beads.

Tape the calotte crimp to your working surface to hold beadwork in position while you braid. An alternative is to pin the calotte crimp to your working surface (if your working surface is suitable, for instance, made of cork board).

Stringing

the slip knots, being careful not to let the braid unravel or the beads slip down the thread. Adjust the length if necessary (taking into account the length that crimps and clasp will add).

8. Pass all three needles through the hole in the second calotte crimp, with the cups facing away from the beads. Press the calotte crimp firmly against the braided strands and tie the three threads together, forming an overhand knot around a needle, as close to the crimp as possible. Use the needle to slide the knot into the calotte crimp.

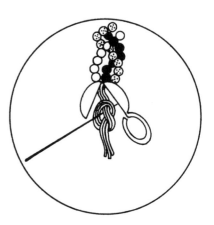

9. Cut the three needles from the thread. Apply a drop of adhesive to the knotted threads in the calotte crimps at each end of the necklace.

10. When the adhesive is dry, cut off excess threads near the knots and use your fingers or pliers to close the calotte crimps.

11. Attach the clasp to the calotte crimp loops. Close the loops.

Voilà! You've learned a new finishing technique and used your imagination to design a striking new necklace.

If you like braiding you'll probably be interested in four-strand braiding, described in the "Other Techniques" section (see page 22). That and the "Finishing Techniques" section at the end of the chapter will give you an idea of the many options for making single and multistrand necklaces and bracelets.

Materials

You'll want to consider the characteristics of your stringing materials as you choose them. See Chapter 11, *Tools and Materials,* for a full description of materials listed below.

BEADS
You can combine beads in countless ways. Try varying bead sizes, colours, materials, shapes and textures until you find a combination that appeals to you. Experiment with symmetrical and asymmetrical arrangements. You can order the beads randomly, in a repeating sequence or according to size. The beads' weight, size and distribution determine how the necklace hangs. Consider these ideas:

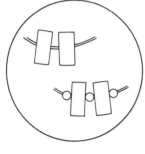

- Two large beads, if placed directly next to each other, may not follow the curve of the necklace. Smaller **spacer** or filler beads placed between larger beads can solve this problem and also showcase the larger beads.

- Use large or special beads as a centrepiece for your necklace.

- Thread **head pins** through beads and attach clusters of dangles to the necklace, separated by sections of single beads. See the dangle earrings project in Chapter 2, *Earrings,* for information on making dangles.

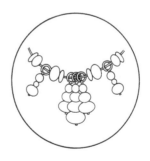

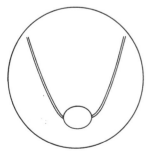

- One large or heavy bead on a long cord will give your necklace a V shape.

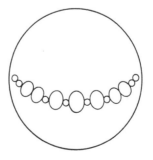

- You can create a U-shaped necklace with a strand of uniform beads or by evenly distributing larger beads throughout the centre of the piece.

When you buy beads, decide on your necklace length and measure the width of the beads you want to use. Divide the necklace length by the width of the beads. This will tell you how many you need.

It's always a good idea to string your beads to see how well they hang before you add the fasteners. (You can temporarily anchor them with slip knots unless you're using wire.)

Check your design by laying out the beads before you string them. Use a loop of masking tape (sticky side out) to hold the beads in position. If you're worried about the tape leaving a residue, an alternative is to lay them on a towel. Or use a **bead board,** which has grooves for arranging beads.

CLASPS

Clasps are metal **findings** that fasten one end of your necklace or bracelet to the other. Make sure the clasp is strong enough to support the weight of the beads. If you're making a bracelet, choose a clasp that you can fasten with one hand. The "Finishing Techniques" section (see page 24) describes how to use clasps and other specialized bead findings to securely finish your strands.

Hook and chain fasteners have two parts: a hook at one end of the beadwork and a chain at the other. This kind of fastener is ideal when the fit of your necklace is important, because you can attach the hook to different chain links to adjust the length.

Screw clasps consist of two parts that screw together, with a loop on each part for attaching the beadwork. The **barrel clasp** and the **torpedo clasp** are named for their shapes.

Snap clasps have two pieces that snap together. The clasp opens only when you press the tab to release the catch. Some styles have several loops for fastening multistrand beadwork.

Spring rings open when you pull back the tab; they have a loop for attaching your beadwork. **Lobster clasps** work the same way, but are shaped like lobster claws. Attach a **tag**, **jump ring** or **split ring** to the other end of the beadwork and insert it into the opening in the spring ring or lobster clasp to close the beadwork.

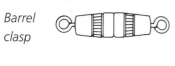

Hook and chain fastener

Barrel clasp

Torpedo clasp

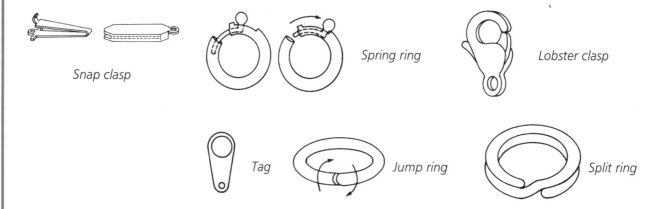

Snap clasp

Spring ring

Lobster clasp

Tag

Jump ring

Split ring

CRIMPS

Use crimps in conjunction with clasps; these metal findings secure the thread, wire or cord at the ends of your necklace or bracelet. Some types that you'll find helpful are **calotte crimps** (also called bead tips), **end springs**, **French crimps** (also called crimp beads), **gimp**, **lace-end crimps** and **stop springs**. Though not technically crimps, **bell caps** and **cones** (used with **eye pins** and **head pins**) and **end spacers** help to secure multiple threads at the ends of your jewellery. The "Finishing

Techniques" section (see page 24) describes how to use crimps and other metal findings to securely finish your bead strands.

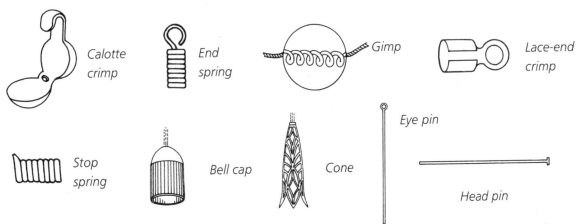

Calotte crimp

End spring

Gimp

Lace-end crimp

Eye pin

Stop spring

Bell cap

Cone

Head pin

THREAD

The beads you plan to use and the effect you want to achieve determine which type of thread, wire or cord to use. Don't underestimate the importance of your thread; choosing the wrong type can have disastrous results, leaving you with a necklace that hangs awkwardly or breaks from the weight of the beads. If you use sharp or heavy beads, for example, you need a strong wire like **tiger-tail**—a strong, nylon-coated steel cable—that won't break. On the other hand, a silk thread will hang less stiffly than monofilament or tiger-tail.

Keep a few alternatives in mind when you string beads of different weights (for a complete description of thread types and uses, see Chapter 11, *Tools and Materials*):

- For lightweight beads and beads with small holes, such as glass **micro beads** and small wood or plastic beads, use **nylon thread** (unwaxed or waxed) or **invisible thread**.
- For medium-weight beads and beads with small to medium holes—such as semiprecious stone beads and small clay, bone or ceramic beads—try **silk thread**, heavier gauge (weight) nylon thread, **elastic thread** or tiger-tail.
- For heavyweight beads and beads with large holes—such as sharp metal or crystal beads, trade beads and large wood or clay beads—use **rattail**, **monofilament fishing line**, leather or cotton **laces**, a heavier gauge of tiger-tail, **fox-tail chain** or **wire**. One type is precoiled steel bracelet and necklace wire.

Choose the thickest thread that will fit through the holes in the beads. The beads will rattle around and shift out of position if the thread is too thin.

Thread can also be a design element if you don't cover it completely with beads. Knot the thread or cord (or use a stop spring or French crimp) to hold beads in position, leaving sections of bare cord.

Always use a single thread unless directed otherwise. To use a single thread, pull a few inches of thread through the needle (just enough so the needle won't fall off). To use a doubled thread, centre the needle on the thread to make two tails of equal length. Many techniques call for a single thread if the thread must pass several times through small bead holes.

*Avoid bending or knotting **tiger-tail**, as this will make your necklace hang awkwardly. Use **French crimps** to secure the tiger-tail to the clasp. (For full information, see the "Finishing Techniques" section on page 24.)*

Rattail is a large cord wrapped in rayon. It has a beautiful, satiny finish, ideal for necklaces with fewer beads and exposed sections of cord. Be careful handing rattail cord, as rough hands or a rough working surface will snag it.

Other Techniques

Bead stringing may seem so simple that no explanations are necessary. Nonetheless, pros have learned tricks over the years that can help you create beautiful jewellery. This section contains information on knotting between beads and creating multiple-strand designs.

KNOTTING BETWEEN BEADS

Knotting between beads is a good practice when you work with pearls or semiprecious stones; it minimizes your loss if the thread breaks. It also prevents the beads from rubbing against each other and separates them to fully display the beauty of each. Knots are also handy for holding beads in position on a lace (see the lace and bead choker project). See Chapter 10, *Basic Knots*, for information on tying different knots.

Some pointers for knotting:
- Use thread thick enough to prevent knots from sliding into bead holes.
- Use *overhand knots* to make small knots and *multiple overhand knots* to make larger knots.
- Allow extra thread if you're knotting a necklace. To determine how long your thread needs to be, measure a section of thread and test it. Knot the beads on and measure the finished product. Compare the finished length to the original length of the thread. Then use the same proportions to calculate the length of thread you need for your completed necklace. As always, add about 15 cm (6 inches) to allow for finishing.

- Position the knots snugly against the beads. Tie a loose overhand or multiple overhand knot. Before you tighten it, slide it into position with a needle.
- Make your knots as tight as possible. The weight of the beads will loosen them later.

Bead Strand Sizing Chart

Beaders use certain terms to describe standard lengths of strung beads. All measurements include the clasp.

Uniform (strand of beads): *all beads are the same size*
Graduated (strand of beads): *beads increase in size from smallest to largest (smallest near clasp)*
Bib: *three or more strands of increasing length*
Dog collar: *three or more strands fitting close to the neck*
Bracelet: *17.5 cm (7 inches)*
Choker: *35–40 cm (14–16 inches)*
Princess: *46 cm (18 inches)*
Matinee: *51–61 cm (20–24 inches)*
Opera: *71–81 cm (28–32 inches)*
Rope: *101 cm (40 inches) or longer (long enough to go around the neck more than once)*
Lariat: *122 cm (48 inches) or longer, not joined at the ends, although the ends may be tied in a knot*

LEATHER LINKS

Another way to separate beads or groups of beads is to make leather links. Use this technique to create unusual necklaces and bracelets. To make links with 1.3 cm (1/2 inch) loops, start with a leather lace 6.3 cm (2 1/2 inches) 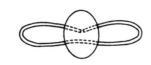 longer than the beads. (This also works nicely with a single bead.) Centre the beads on the leather, place a drop of **adhesive** on the end of the lace and insert 0.6 cm (1/4 inch) back into the bead. Repeat at the other side. For subsequent links, loop the lace through the link you just made before inserting it into a bead. At the ends of the necklace or bracelet, loop one side of the last link through the previous link and attach a lace-end crimp or end spring to the loose leather end. Alter the length of the leather pieces to make different-sized loops.

*As an alternative to knotting between beads, filigreed or other ornate **bead caps**, threaded on to enclose the bead on both sides, give a beautiful effect and also protect the beads.*

MULTIPLE-STRAND JEWELLERY

You can use multiple strands to create endless jewellery variations. Strands can be graduated or equal in length. Intersperse larger beads on strands of small beads, or alternate seed and bugle beads. Try twisting or braiding strands together. Or join multiple strands of small beads by periodically passing all the strands through a larger bead or a **spacer bar**.

The second project uses the three-strand braiding technique. This technique is useful for braiding larger numbers of strands; simply divide the strands into three groups and treat each group as a single strand. The same applies to four-strand braiding.

To twist multiple strands of beads together, divide the strands into two groups joined at one end. Twist each group of strands in the same direction. Then twist the two groups around each other in the opposite direction.

FOUR-STRAND BRAIDING

Use this technique to braid four single strands of beads; anchor the strands together at one end. For the first sequence, pass the left strand over the strand next to it. Pass the right strand over the two middle strands. Pass the right strand over the strand next to it, then pass the left strand over the two middle strands.

The second sequence is the opposite of the first. Pass the right strand over the strand next to it, then pass the left strand over the two middle strands; pass the left strand over the strand next to it, then pass the right strand over the two middle strands.

Continue alternating the first and second sequence until you reach the desired length, braiding as tightly or loosely as you wish.

*The finished braid is always shorter than the strands you begin with, but the amount of shrinkage depends on how tightly you braid and how large the beads are. Tie a **slip knot** at the end of each strand of beads when you're ready to begin braiding so you can later add or remove beads if necessary.*

Finishing Techniques

You can use various techniques and findings for finishing strung jewellery. Choose your technique to suit the number of strands, thread type and length of necklace.

SINGLE STRAND

Try the following findings and finishing techniques for single-strand jewellery:

- If your thread is lightweight (silk or nylon), put the end through the hole in a **calotte crimp**, then through a small seed bead that fits inside the calotte. Pull the thread tight, knot the thread around the bead (if the thread is too thick to fit through a seed bead, just tie it in a large knot) and—without cutting the thread—apply adhesive to the knot.

  Pass the thread back out through the hole in the calotte and back through the first bead. Then tie a knot around the necklace thread, pass it through the next bead, knot again and pass it through a few more beads (note that the space between the beads in the diagram is exaggerated for effect). Apply adhesive to the knots and cut off excess thread. Hide the knots (if small enough) and the thread tip inside the bead holes. Press the calotte crimp shut using your fingers or **pliers**. Attach the clasp to the calotte crimps.

- If your thread is heavier (tiger-tail or monofilament), put it through a **French crimp**, loop it through a clasp loop, jump ring or split ring, and insert it back through the crimp. Pull the thread tight and use pliers or a **crimping tool** to squeeze the crimp shut. For an extra-secure fastening, place a small drop of adhesive inside the

  French crimp before closing it. Pass the thread through an inch of beads and cut off the excess, taking care not to leave a tail sticking out between the beads that might jab the wearer.

- When you use a French crimp, the thread or wire shows where it passes through the clasp loop. To cover the thread use 1.3 cm to 2 cm (1/2 inch to 3/4 inch) of **gimp**. (The

section of thread covered with gimp is shown as striped in the diagram.) Put the gimp on the thread before looping through the clasp or ring. Bend the gimp to form a loop, centre this loop in the clasp's loop, then pass the thread or wire back through the crimp and into the beads.

- For thicker cord or leather, use **lace-end crimps** or **end springs**. Squeeze the crimp or spring shut over the end of the cord and attach the clasp to the loop in the crimp or spring.

- Make your own fastener out of beads. Put a large bead at one end, and at the other end, a loop of smaller beads that will fit over the larger bead. If you like, use smaller beads to cover the thread at the sides of the large bead. Use French crimps or knot the threads between beads (as described on the previous page) to secure the threads.

- For continuous strands long enough to fit over your head, you needn't use a clasp. Tie a *square knot* to join the ends. Then pass the ends back through the first bead on each side, knot them around the necklace thread, pass them through the next bead and knot again. Pass the thread through a few more beads, cut off the excess and apply adhesive to the knots.

- For an adjustable closure that lets you vary the strand's length, create a chain-end out of beads and **eye pins**. Thread a bead on an eye pin and form the straight end into a loop. Make as many eye pin-and-bead links as you need to create the length of chain you want, linking them with the loops. Attach the chain to one end of the strand and use a hook at the other end. See the dangle earrings project (page 28) for more information on bending wire to form loops.

- A *sliding knot* offers another way to create an adjustable closure for leather laces or other cords. See Chapter 10, *Basic Knots*, for information about making sliding knots.

MULTIPLE STRANDS

You can adapt single-strand finishing techniques to suit multistrand jewellery. Also try these ideas:

- French crimps let you use one crimp for two threads; just make sure the threads are side by side, not overlapping, when you squeeze the crimp shut. Otherwise the threads may shift, causing the crimp to slip.

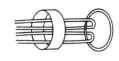

- Use an **end spacer** that has a hole or loop for each strand or pair of strands. Use French crimps (and gimp, if you wish) or calotte crimps before attaching the strands to the end spacer. Attach the clasp to the side of the end spacer having a single hole or loop.

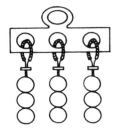

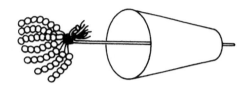

- Use **cones** and **head pins** to conceal the ends of multiple strands. Knot the threads at one end together and cut off the excess thread. Bend the head pin near the head. Push the tip of the head pin through the knot and position the knot at the bend in the pin. (If you like, secure the threads to the head pin with adhesive.) Pull the tip of the pin through the hole in the cone and cut off excess wire, leaving 0.6 cm to 1.3 cm (1/4 inch to 1/2 inch) to form a loop. Loop the end of the wire and attach the loop directly to a clasp, or attach it to a single strand of beads. Repeat at the other end.

- To fasten multiple laces at the end of a necklace or bracelet, use an **end spring** made to hold two or three laces. Put the laces inside the spring. Place your pliers over the end of the coiled wire so the wire end will bite into the lace, and squeeze it shut.

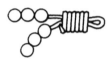

Chapter Two
Earrings

Earrings must be among the most popular jewellery of all time. Today they're as fashionable as ever. You can make beaded earrings that are simple, elegant or funky, in delicate metal tones or a riot of colour. Whatever your style, earrings can express it. You don't even have to pierce your ears; earring findings are available for pierced and unpierced ears.

Beaded earrings are fast, easy and inexpensive to create. They make great gifts, and a few new pairs of earrings can help you feel as though you have a whole new wardrobe. You can use any beading technique in this book to create your own unique earring designs. In fact, scaling down a technique to suit earrings is a great way to learn it. Earrings are quick to put together; you'll soon see whether you like the results. A wide variety of earring and jewellery findings can help you create a professionally finished look.

This chapter begins with a simple earrings project to get you used to working with some basic tools and earring findings. The second, more difficult, project introduces you to bead weaving. The next section describes specialized materials used for earrings; the final section offers additional earring techniques to stir your imagination.

Dangle Earrings Project

This project shows you how to make a simple pair of earrings, using beads and head pins (wire pins with a flat head at one end) to create two dangles with loops at the top for attaching your earring findings. The earrings in the photograph are made of green "fossil" stone beads and gold-coloured disks; they cost less than two dollars to make. You can choose any colour and any number of beads.

SHOPPING LIST

- beads
- 2 head pins (plus extras for practice)
  Note: Make sure the head pins are long enough to leave at least 0.6 cm to 0.8 cm (1/4 inch to 5/16 inch) of wire to form a loop after you put the beads on.
- 2 kidney ear wires (or another type of **earring finding**; choose a type with a loop for attaching the dangle)

TOOL KIT

- round-nose pliers
- tape measure
- wire snips
- needle-nose pliers (optional)
- fine metal file (optional)
- safety glasses (optional

BEADING

1. Arrange your beads on a head pin, with the head at the bottom of the dangle.

2. Position the round-nose pliers on the wire as close as possible to the beads. Bend the wire slightly to one side by gripping the wire firmly with the pliers, then pushing the wire inside the top beads toward the pliers with your finger.

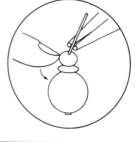

If the head pin is made of a soft metal the pliers may leave marks on the pin, even though round-nose pliers have smooth jaws. The degree of softness or hardness is called "pliability," and varies from manufacturer to manufacturer. One advantage of softer wire is that it's easier to bend.

In step 3, if your head pin is made of a harder wire, it could be difficult to bend the end of the wire with your finger. If so, position the pliers near the end of the head pin and push against the beads to roll the wire into a loop around the pliers. You may find it helpful to brace the earring against your working surface. Reposition the pliers as often as necessary.

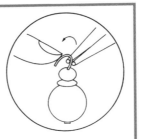

3. Bend the wire around the round tip of the pliers, forming a loop. Again, grip the wire firmly with the pliers and bend the wire by pushing it with your finger.

4. The end of the wire should just reach the spot where the wire emerges from the top bead. If it doesn't, make one of these adjustments:

- If the wire is too long, use wire snips to trim it. First you may need to pull the end of the wire forward, away from the beginning of the loop, to make room for the wire snips. (Or measure the excess length, open the loop and remove the beads from the head pin. Use wire snips to cut excess length from a new head pin, file the cut edge smooth, and begin again at step 1.)
- If the wire is too short to form a complete loop around the tip of your pliers, you have several options. Grip the wire from the side near the beginning of the loop—you may need needle-nose pliers for a good grip—and use your fingers or another pair of pliers to pull the end of the wire toward the beads, making a smaller loop. Or open the loop, take the beads off and start over with a longer pin or fewer beads.

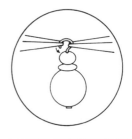

5. Once you're satisfied with the loop, attach the dangle to your earring finding:

- On kidney ear wires, position the loop in the kink of the ear wire, then close the top of the kink with your fingers or pliers.
- On other kinds of earring findings, open the finding loop by twisting the end of the wire sideways. (Don't pull it outward or the wire will weaken and the loop will lose its round shape.) Insert the dangle loop into the finding loop and close the finding loop.

6. Repeat these steps to make the second earring.

Now you've made a beautiful, inexpensive pair of earrings, and you've mastered the art of making a simple wire loop.

Earrings

Earrings

Fringed Earrings Project

This project shows you how to use bead weaving techniques to make basic fringed earrings. Although this earrings project will take longer than the first one, you'll find these one-of-a-kind earrings fun to make.

Each earring (see photograph) has a foundation of bugle beads and seed beads woven together to form a triangle, and a loop for attaching the earring finding. The fringe is made up of seven dangles with increasing numbers of seed beads; this gives the earring its lovely tapered shape. Use any colours you wish, with thread to match, but remember at first it's easier to stick to fewer colours. Once you gain expertise, you can use several colours and experiment with different shapes, beads and patterns.

This technique also works well with invisible thread, a transparent nylon thread that resembles fine fishing line but is more flexible. It's available at most fabric shops.

SHOPPING LIST
- 268 size 10° seed beads
- 70—5 mm bugle beads
- nylon thread
- 2 earring findings (choose a type with a loop for attaching the beadwork)

TOOL KIT
- beading needle (threader optional)
- scissors
- file (use a fine metal file)
- needle-nose pliers
- tape measure

MEASURING YOUR THREAD

Each earring requires approximately 2 metres (2 yards) of thread. If you run out of thread, add more as described in Chapter 9, *Solutions to Common Beading Problems.*

BEADING

Choose beads that are uniform in size. If the bugle beads have sharp or irregular ends, file them smooth (using a fine metal file) before you begin beading. Choose beads with large holes; the thread must pass through them several times. It's important to keep your beads tightly together and your thread taut as you add beads to your foundation row, which forms the base of your earring and must be strong enough to carry the weight of the fringe.

Bugle bead foundation row using the ladder stitch

1. Place your needle 10 cm (about 4 inches) from the end of the thread and use it to pick up two bugle beads. Push them down the thread to about 15 cm (6 inches) from the end.

2. Pass the needle through the two bugle beads again, in the same direction as before, and pull the thread tight. The two beads now lie side by side. The thread should emerge from the bottom of the second bugle bead.

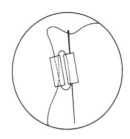

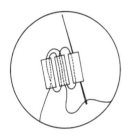

3. Add another bugle bead. Pass the needle down through the top of the second bugle bead and then up through the third bugle bead.

4. Pick up a bugle bead. Pass the needle up through the third bugle bead and down through the one you just added.

5. Repeat steps 3 and 4 to add three more bugle beads. When done, you should have seven bugle beads in a tight side-by-side row.

Be sure you don't kink the thread. Even a kink hidden inside a bead can come back to haunt you by later loosening, leaving an ugly loop of thread protruding from your beadwork.

6. Strengthen your foundation row by passing the needle back through all the bugle beads. Your thread should now emerge from the top of the very first bugle bead.

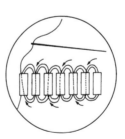

Seed bead triangle using the brick stitch

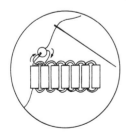

7. Pick up a seed bead with the needle. Pass the needle under the top pair of threads, between the first two bugle beads, and push it back through the seed bead.

8. Pick up another seed bead. Pass the needle under the top pair of threads between the second and third bugle beads and back up through the seed bead. Repeat to complete the first row of six seed beads.

9. Continue in this way, taking the needle through the loop of thread between beads to add the next rows of first five, then four, three and two seed beads.

Top loop (to attach the earring finding)

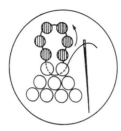

10. Starting from the right-hand seed bead in the final row, pick up six seed beads, then pass the needle through the final row of two seed beads in the triangle to form a loop at the tip.

11. Pass the needle through the six seed beads and final row again, then down the outer left column of seed beads, then through the first bugle bead in the foundation row.

Fringe

12. Pick up thirteen beads in this order: four seed beads, one bugle bead, three seed beads, one bugle bead, one seed bead, one bugle bead, one seed bead, one bugle bead.

13. Pass the needle back up through all the beads of the dangle except the bottom three. Hold the bottom seed bead and pull the thread tight. The dangle should be straight, with no thread showing.

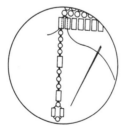

14. Pass the needle up through the same foundation bugle bead the thread emerged from and then down through the next foundation bugle bead.

15. Repeat steps 12 through 14 to add six more dangles, but add an extra seed bead to the second group of seed beads in each successive dangle to create a diagonal shape. That is, four seed beads instead of three in the second dangle, five seed beads in the third dangle and so on. The last dangle will have nine seed beads in its second group of seed beads.

In tight spots, use pliers to pull the needle through beads. Be sure to grasp the needle close to where it exits the beads, not down at the tip, to avoid breaking the needle.

FINISHING

1. Finish your earring by passing your needle up through the last foundation bugle bead and up the outer right column of seed beads in the triangle.

2. Knot the thread between the top two beads in the triangle, using an *overhand knot* or *double half-hitch* (see methods in Chapter 10, *Basic Knots*). Weave the thread back down into the triangle, pulling the knot inside a bead so it doesn't show. Cut off excess thread.

3. Weave the other tail of thread through a few beads in the triangle and cut off excess thread. Take care that no thread ends are showing.

4. Adjust the hang of the earring before you attach the earring finding to the top loop. Normally you'll attach the finding between the third and fourth seed beads, but if the earring doesn't hang straight when suspended from this position, you may want to put the finding one bead to the left or right. Use pliers to open and close the loop in the earring finding.

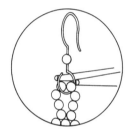

Repeat these steps to make the second earring, but make sure that when you attach the finding the fringe tapers the opposite way.

Now you've made an attractive pair of earrings and you've learned two off-loom weaving techniques: the *ladder stitch* and the *brick stitch*. See Chapter 3, *Off-Loom Weaving,* for more information on bead weaving methods. The "Fringed Earring Variations" section (see page 40) may give you ideas for adapting the basic technique to create your own designer earrings.

Earrings

Materials

Many jewellery findings are designed especially for making earrings. An **earring finding** is any metal material used to attach the beadwork part of an earring to the ear. This section describes these and other materials that are handy for making earrings. The "Using Jewellery Findings" section later in this chapter describes how to use them.

Bead cap

Bead cap. A metal disk with a hole in the centre, curved to fit snugly against a bead. Use a bead cap at the bottom of an earring dangle as an alternative to a **stopper bead**, if an **eye pin** or **head pin** would slip right through a large hole in the bottom bead.

Bell cap

Bell cap. A metal finding shaped like a bell, used with **eye pins** and **head pins** to join multiple loops neatly. **Cones** perform the same function, but are cone-shaped. Some bell caps have a loop at one end and flexible claws at the other end for attaching beads without holes.

Cabochon. A glass, acrylic or semiprecious stone with a rounded top and a flat back. Use adhesive to attach cabochons to **ear posts**.

Calotte crimp

Calotte crimp (bead tip). A knot cover made of a hinged cup with an attached loop. Use it to attach dangles to earring findings.

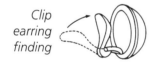

Clip earring finding

Clip earring finding. A clip finding, for unpierced ears or heavy earrings, does not go through the ear but clips onto the lower earlobe. It may have a loop for attaching beadwork, a flat surface to glue stones onto or a woven mesh or screened disk to sew the beads to. Bead shops sometimes sell small rubber pieces that you can glue to the back of clips to make them more comfortable.

Ear hoop

Ear hoop. A thin wire hoop that is inserted into the ear.

Ear post (stud). This wire post is inserted directly through a pierced ear and held in place with a **clutch** (butterfly). It may have a loop for attaching dangles, a flat pad for fastening flat-backed beads, a cup and prong for securing half-drilled beads, or claws to hold a bead in position.

Ear post (stud) with clutch (butterfly)

End spacer

End spacer. A metal finding with multiple loops or holes on one side and one loop or hole on the other side. Attach your earring dangles to the multiple loops or holes and attach the other side to your earring finding.

Eye pin. A flexible pin with a loop at one end. After you thread beads onto the pin, form a loop with the straight end. This creates a dangle with a loop at either end; you can attach additional dangles to one loop and use the other loop to attach the beadwork to your earring finding.

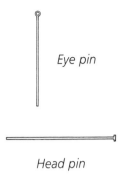

Eye pin

Head pin. A wire pin with a flat head at one end. After you thread beads onto the pin, form a loop with the straight end to attach the dangle to your earring finding.

Head pin

Jump ring. A fine loop of wire with ends that press together. Use jump rings as an intermediate loop between dangles and your earring finding. **Split rings** are similar but have overlapping ends.

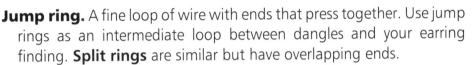

Jump ring

Kidney ear wire. A thin wire loop that fits through a pierced ear. The top is rounded and the back hooks into a bend in the front. Position the loop of your beadwork in the kink, then press the kink closed to hold the beadwork in place.

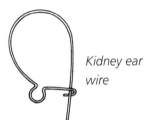

Kidney ear wire

Screened disk earring finding. This earring finding has two parts: a curved disk with holes and a back piece with an earring finding attached. After you anchor the beads to the disk by threading through the holes, clip the back part on and bend the claws to hold it in place.

Screw earring finding. Findings that screw onto the back of the earlobe for unpierced ears or heavy earrings. Some have loops for attaching dangles, others have a flat piece for setting a stone with adhesive.

Screw earring finding

Shepherd's hook ear wire. A thin wire hook for pierced ears, with loops for suspending beadwork.

Shepherd's hook ear wire

Triangle (bail or bale). A triangular metal finding with two straight prongs that you insert into a bead to hold it securely. Loop the earring finding through the top of the triangle.

Wire spirals. Wire coils that you form yourself to create an unusual earring shape. You can cover them with beads or just space a few beads along the spiral.

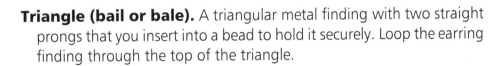

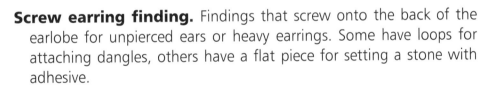

Triangle

Earrings

Other Techniques

Beaded earrings generally have two parts: a piece of beadwork and an earring finding that attaches the beadwork to your ear. You can use just about any beading technique to make earrings, and your bead store carries many jewellery findings to give your earrings a professional finish. This section describes many different ways to make the beadwork and how to attach it to the earring finding. These ideas can get you started, but you'll probably think of many other ways to combine basic beading techniques in your own designs.

USING JEWELLERY FINDINGS

Jewellery findings help you make earrings like a pro. Your earrings can look even better than store-bought earrings, because your choice of colours and style will suit your tastes exactly. The dangle earrings project at the beginning of this chapter shows you how to make a simple dangle earring by threading beads onto a **head pin** and forming a loop with the straight part of the pin.

Here are some other ways you can incorporate jewellery findings into your earring designs (see page 38 for methods of making your own jewellery findings):

- Create dangles by putting beads onto head pins. Attach them to another dangle made with an **eye pin** and attach the top loop in the eye pin dangle to your earring finding.

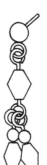

- Make a delicate teardrop earring by centring small beads (an odd number works best) on a doubled nylon thread. Pass both ends of the thread through another bead to form a teardrop shape. Pass the threads through the hole in a calotte crimp and knot them around a seed bead inside the crimp. Secure the knot with a drop of adhesive. Close the crimp and attach its loop to your earring finding.

- Thread beads onto a **wire spiral** that you make yourself (see "Making Your Own Jewellery Findings," later in this chapter, for methods of working with wire).

- Put beads or dangles directly onto **ear hoops**. After you close the hoop, crimp the insertable end of the wire with needle-nose pliers to secure the wire.

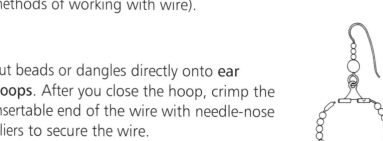

• Connect the beadwork to your earring finding with fancy wire **scrolls** or **S-links** that you make yourself (see "Making Your Own Jewellery Findings," later in this chapter, for more information).

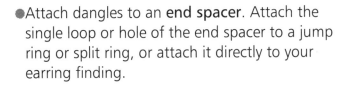

• Squeeze the ends of a **triangle** into a large bead. Attach the triangle to an eye pin dangle, to a **jump ring** or **split ring**, or directly to your earring finding.

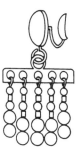

• Attach dangles to an **end spacer**. Attach the single loop or hole of the end spacer to a jump ring or split ring, or attach it directly to your earring finding.

 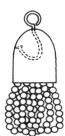

• Make cone-and-tassel earrings by threading several loops (of the same or varying lengths) of seed beads. Use an *overhand knot* to tie the threads together near the beads. Cut off excess thread. Bend a head pin near the head and insert the pin through the knot, which will rest in the bend of the pin. (If you like, secure the thread to the pin using **adhesive**.) Pull the end of the pin through a **bell cap** or **cone**. Cut off excess wire, leaving about 0.6 cm to 1.3 cm (1/4 inch to 1/2 inch) and use pliers to form a loop in the remaining wire.

*When you attach beads to ear posts, use a fine metal **file** to roughen the flat surfaces of the ear post and the bead (when using a stone bead, just roughen the ear post). Then clean both surfaces. Adhesive will bond better to these clean, slightly rough surfaces. If the ear post has no prong or claws to secure the bead, use a toothpick or pin to apply additional adhesive around the edge where the bead joins to the backing.*

• Glue **cabochons** onto flat-backed **ear posts**.

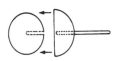

• Attach beads with partially-drilled holes onto ear posts that have a cup and prong.

• Attach semiprecious stones to ear posts that have claws around the edges of the pad, then bend the claws to hold the stone in place.

Earrings

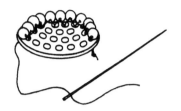

●Sew beads onto a **screened disk** earring. Remove the disk from its backing before attaching the beads. Thread on enough beads to completely cover the disk. (One way to do this is to attach a circle of beads around the outer edge, then work inward.) Keep knots and threads hidden at the back of the disk. Add dangles if you wish. Finally, apply adhesive to the knots. Using needle-nose pliers, attach the disk to its backing by bending the claws to hold the disk firmly in place. Use the same method to attach circular pieces of beadwork to screened disk earrings (see Chapter 3, *Off-Loom Weaving*, for methods of weaving circular beadwork pieces).

Making your own jewellery findings

Combining wire with beads is an ancient art form. You can make your own jewellery findings and blend simple wire shapes with beads to create truly one-of-a-kind earrings. The dangle earrings project at the beginning of this chapter shows you how easy it is to form a loop at the end of a head pin to make a simple earring dangle.

You can use the same skills to make your own eye pins, jump rings and other findings. This section describes some simple wire findings that you can make to attach beads to your earring findings. All you need is **wire**, **wire snips**, a fine metal **file** and a pair of **pliers**. With a little practice, you'll think of all kinds of ways to incorporate wire shapes into your beaded jewellery designs.

First, some general tips for working with wire:
●Use 18- to 22-gauge wire to make jewellery findings.
●Use pliers with smooth jaws (or wrap the tips of your pliers with masking tape) to avoid marring the wire. (If the wire is soft, even smooth-jawed pliers may dent it.)
●Use metal cleaner to clean the wire (steel wool works, too, for brass and copper wire).
●File cut ends smooth with an even, forward-sliding stroke.

Eye pins. Cut a length of wire 1.3 cm (1/2 inch) longer than you want the finished eye pin. File the ends smooth. Position round-nose pliers about 0.6 cm (1/4 inch) from the end of the wire. Using your fingers, bend the short end of wire around the tip of the pliers to form a loop. (If this is too difficult, place the pliers at the end of the wire and bend the long end around the tip.) Place the pliers at the neck of the loop and bend the long end in the opposite direction to centre the wire beneath the loop.

Jump rings and split rings. To make two jump rings, wind the wire tightly around a cylindrical object (knitting needle, nail, pencil, wood dowel or round-nose pliers tip), until you have two complete circles. Remove the coiled wire, and cut off the excess (the wire after the second circle) with wire snips. Cut through the middle point of the wire, to separate the two circles. File the ends smooth. To make oval jump rings, wrap the wire around two nails or dowels placed side by side. To make a **split ring**, follow these instructions but don't cut through the circles.

cut here

cut here

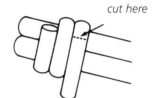
cut here

Scrolls and S-links. Try forming your wire into interesting shapes as an alternative to jump rings and split rings. You can thread beads onto the scrolls and S-links or just use them to link your beadwork to the earring finding.

Here are a few ideas:

Triangles. Cut a 2 cm to 2.5 cm (3/4 inch to 1 inch) length of wire and file the ends smooth. Form a 90-degree angle in the middle of the wire by placing it so half extends over the edge of your working table. Press the overhanging wire downward with your fingers. Use flat-nose pliers to bend the ends of the wire inward.

90°

Wire spirals. Cut a 5 cm (2 inch) length of wire and file the ends smooth. Make a small loop at one end of the wire. Wind the wire around a cone-shaped object or gently curve it into a spiral with round-nose pliers. Add beads to cover all but the last 0.6 cm (1/4 inch) of the wire, then form a loop in the end to hold the beads in place. Or strategically scatter a few beads throughout the spiral, holding them in position with a small drop of adhesive or with **French crimps**.

FRINGED EARRING VARIATIONS

Fringed earrings never seem to lose their popularity. This chapter's second project shows you how to make basic fringed earrings. They have a triangular foundation of woven seed and bugle beads, with bead fringes attached to the base and a loop of beads at the top for attaching an earring finding. This section describes different ways of constructing the foundation and attaching dangles. Mix and match the foundations and fringes to create earrings that have your own special touch.

Here are some ideas for altering the basic fringed earring foundation:

- Vary the width of the first foundation row; use five or nine bugle beads instead of seven. An odd number usually works best
- Try using groups of three seed beads instead of bugle beads in the first row of the foundation.
- Alternate bugle beads with seed beads in the first row of the foundation. Use enough seed beads to equal the length of the bugle beads (usually three or four, but the number may vary depending on the size of your bugle and seed beads).

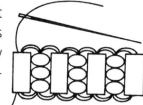

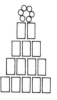

- Use bugle beads instead of seed beads in the upper rows of the foundation. It's best to use shorter bugle beads because they're less fragile. They also result in a triangle with more pleasing proportions than longer bugle beads.

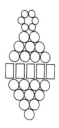

- Add another triangle below the first row of the foundation to create a diamond shape.

- Invert the triangle and hang fringes off the sides.

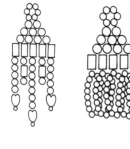

The dangles can also be altered to create many different effects:

- Taper the fringe so it's longest in the middle and shorter at both edges.
- Incorporate different combinations of bugle beads and seed beads, or add large beads or porcupine quills.
- Make loop dangles instead of a single strand.
- Use loops of increasing length, with the ends attached to the foundation at opposite sides.
- Make two foundation triangles, join the triangles with seed beads between each row and connect them with looped dangles.

ADVANCED FOUNDATIONS

You can adapt any beading technique to make earrings. This is a good way to try a new technique on a small, quickly finished piece. This section discusses some additional ways to construct beaded earring foundations. Keep in mind that this section describes *advanced* techniques—they are more complicated than the techniques presented earlier in the chapter! Some foundations look beautiful by themselves; others look incomplete without dangles. After you read the suggestions below, read the other technique chapters in this book and let your imagination run wild. Just make sure your design includes a loop for attaching the earring finding.

Porcupine quills are used in many traditional native American designs. Use thick quills of uniform size. Cut off the quill tips before stringing.

- Use the *peyote stitch* to make an 8 cm (3 inch) tube and form it into a circle. If you wish, insert a hoop-shaped wire into the tube before joining the ends to help the foundation maintain a circular shape. Add a loop of seed beads at the top of the circle, then weave through the beads until you reach the spot where you want to add a dangle. Add the beads for the dangle, then continue weaving through the circle to the next spot where you want a dangle. (This foundation also looks attractive without dangles.) See pages 51 and 60 for information about doing the peyote stitch.

- Make a fan-shaped foundation by adding seed beads between the tops of the bugle beads. Construct the fan as described for making the foundation row of the fringed earrings project, but add one or two seed beads before you string on the second bugle bead. Pass the thread back through the first bugle bead, the seed bead(s), and the second bugle bead. Now the thread is emerging from the bottom of the second bugle bead, and you add a bugle bead first, then the seed bead(s), so the seed beads are always at the top. Keep adding beads until you've formed a half-circle. Add a row of three seed beads beneath each of the two bottom bugle beads and connect the two sides of the half-circle with loops of beads. Don't forget to add a loop of seed beads at the top of the foundation for the earring finding.

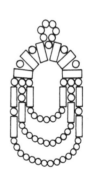

- Make a rectangular foundation with three horizontal bugle beads in the middle and three vertical bugle beads at each side. (Depending on the length of your bugle beads you may need to adjust the number of beads in each section.) Begin by making the central horizontal row of three bugle beads. With the thread emerging from either end bugle bead, add a bugle bead and pass the thread through the bugle bead at the other end of the central row. Repeat to add a bugle bead on the other side of the central row. Pass the needle through the first vertical bugle bead you added, then add

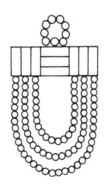

two more bugle beads next to it. Weave through the beads until the thread is emerging from the single vertical bead on the other side, and add two more beads to complete the rectangle. Add a row of seed beads above the top central bugle bead and attach a loop to the seed beads. String loops to connect the two sets of vertical bugle beads.

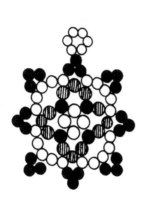

●Another advanced foundation is the mandala (a woven circular shape). To make a simple mandala, begin with a circle of four seed beads. Add a bead between each of the first four beads, to form corners. Then add a loop of three beads between each of the corner beads. Connect the middle beads in the three-bead loops with loops of five beads. Add a circlet of three beads to the middle beads of the three-bead loops and the middle beads of the five-bead loops (eight circlets in all). Add a loop to attach the earring finding or attach the finding to an outer circlet.

●Use **ear hoops** to make dream catcher earrings. Some ear hoops, called **pinched hoops**, are made especially for dream catchers, with little grooves in the hoop for securing the web cord. See Chapter 6, *Other Things You Can Bead*, for information about making dream catchers.

Chapter Three

Off-Loom Weaving

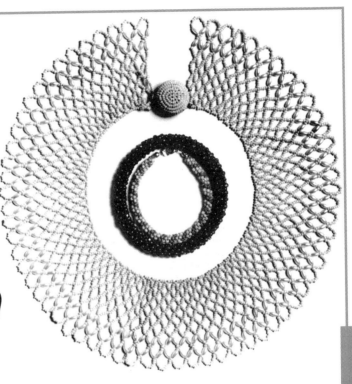

Bead weaving is a way of passing thread back and forth through the beads to create a wonderful beaded fabric effect.

You've probably seen loom woven beadwork, but did you know that there are also many weaving techniques that don't require a loom? You can achieve various effects from delicate, lacy collars to solid creations that resemble loom woven beadwork. Off-loom weaving lets you create striking designs through your choice and placement of different colours of beads.

Off-loom weaving is most commonly used to form simple chains of beads for rings, bracelets and necklaces, or wider pieces for chokers, armbands and wristbands. But once you've tried some techniques you'll see the possibilities for using this method to make brooches, earrings, barrettes, hairbands, beaded belts, vests, purses, wall hangings and more. The seed bead—a small bead available in hundreds of colours—is usually used with bead weaving techniques, but you can also add bugle beads and larger beads.

This chapter begins with three sample projects to show you basic off-loom weaving techniques: the daisy chain, netting and the peyote stitch. The fourth section offers variations plus many additional techniques. The final section describes how to finish your woven beadwork.

Daisy Chain Bracelet Project

The daisy chain or *flower chain* is one of the most basic and universal off-loom stitches. It's ideal for making simple but charming bracelets, rings and necklaces. The pattern you'll use creates a narrow bracelet made of circles of eight seed beads surrounding a single bead in a different colour. The colours of inner and outer beads alternate for each circle (see photograph), so the bracelet actually does look like a chain of flowers.

If you like the daisy chain stitch, after this project you can vary it to produce different patterns and wider or more complex bands. "Daisy Chain Variations" (page 56) offers suggestions.

In the meantime, use this simple pattern to get the feel of off-loom weaving. Don't worry about getting everything perfect the first time. If you make a mistake, you can always go back and correct it. If there are points you don't understand, plunge ahead anyway. Moves which seem puzzling at first will soon become clear.

Choose beads in two colours that go well together; select thread that matches one colour. For simplicity the directions call one colour A and the other colour B.

Many off-loom weaving techniques call for a single thread if the thread must pass several times through small bead holes. To use a single thread, pull a few inches of thread through the needle (just enough so the needle won't fall off). To use a doubled thread, centre the needle on the thread to make two tails of equal length.

SHOPPING LIST

- size 10° seed beads (109 colour A and 100 colour B)

  Note: These quantities yield a 17 cm (6.75 inch) bracelet. You may need more or fewer beads if your bracelet is a different length or if you use a different size of seed beads.

- nylon thread
- 1 clasp (choose a type you can fasten with one hand)
- 2 calotte crimps (also called bead tips)

TOOL KIT

- beeswax
- beading needle (threader optional)
- scissors
- needle-nose pliers
- tape measure
- adhesive

If your beads get mixed up, try using a guitar pick, credit card or similar piece of stiff plastic to sort them.

MEASURING YOUR THREAD

The beadwork should be 1.3 cm (1/2 inch) shorter than the wearer's wrist measurement to allow for the clasp, which adds about 2 cm (3/4 inch). The extra 0.7 cm (1/4 inch) allows for a comfortable fit. This technique takes approximately 13.3 cm (5 1/4 inches) of thread for each 2.5 cm (1 inch) of finished beadwork. Since it's always better to have too much than too little, make your thread six times the planned length of the finished beadwork. Then add 30 cm (12 inches) for the finishing knots.

If you miscalculate and come up short, or if this long thread makes it difficult to work, add more thread when you need it. For instructions on adding thread, see Chapter 9, *Solutions to Common Beading Problems.* If you use unwaxed thread, wax it to prevent tangling.

BEADING

1. Put a needle onto one end of your thread and tie a *slip knot* about 7.6 cm (3 inches) from the other end. See Chapter 10, *Basic Knots*, for instructions on tying slip knots and other knots used for this project.

2. Use the needle to pick up seven beads in this order: AABAAAA. Slide them down the thread to the slip knot.

3. Pass the needle (in the opposite direction) back through the first two A beads.

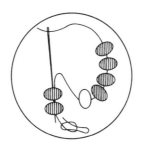

4. Pull the thread tight so the beads form a loop.

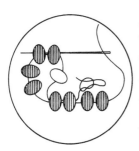

5. Thread two A beads and pass the needle back through the two A beads on the opposite side of the daisy from the slip knot, as shown in the diagram. Pull the thread tight to form a circle of eight A beads around the single B bead. You have just created your first daisy.

6. Thread two B beads and pass the needle through the same two A beads you passed the needle through in step 5. Pull tight. Then pass the needle through the two B beads again in the same direction. (Beginners often miss this step.) Now the first two beads of your second daisy are attached to the end of the first daisy.

This bead weaving technique uses a single thread, so if the amount of thread is too long for you to work with comfortably, move the needle closer to the beadwork. This doubling effectively shortens the thread. Move the needle back along the thread as you work so you don't weave in the tail by mistake.

If your beadwork doesn't look right, compare it to the beadwork in the corresponding diagram. If the loop of beads has twisted the wrong way, just twist it around so that your beadwork matches the diagram.

Off-Loom Weaving

Off-Loom Weaving

7. Thread five more beads in this order: ABBBB, and pass the needle back (in the opposite direction) through the two B beads attached in step 6. Pull tight.

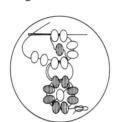

8. Thread two B beads and pass the needle through the two B beads on the end of the new daisy directly opposite the first two attached in step 6, as shown in the diagram. Pull tight. Now you have completed the second daisy.

9. Repeat steps 6 through 8, reversing the colours for each daisy. Continue until you have reached the desired length—the wearer's wrist measurement less 1.3 cm (1/2 inch)—for your bracelet's beadwork portion. Try to finish with a circle of the same colour as your first.

ONE-THREAD FINISHING TECHNIQUE

Now you have a piece of daisy chain beadwork with a single thread at each end. To add the calotte crimps and clasp, start with the end that still has a needle attached:

1. Push the needle through the hole in a calotte crimp with the cups of the calotte facing away from the beadwork. Pick up a seed bead small enough to fit inside the calotte.

2. Pass the needle back out of the hole in the calotte and weave it through the last circle in the beadwork, then back into the calotte and bead. Repeat.

3. Use the needle and thread to tie three half-hitches around the loops of thread that go through the bead in the calotte. Pull the thread tight and apply a drop of adhesive to the knotted thread.

4. Untie the slip knot and place the needle on the thread at the other end. Repeat steps 1 through 3 to attach the other calotte crimp to the beadwork.

5. When the adhesive is dry, cut off excess thread close to the knots. Use your fingers or pliers to close the calotte crimps. Attach the clasps to the loops in the calotte crimps and close the loops.

You've just learned an off-loom weaving stitch. You've also made a pretty bracelet for yourself or a friend.

It is important to keep your daisies tightly formed as you proceed. All beads should be touching, with no thread showing in between. Loose thread will spoil the shape of the chain and prove difficult to tighten later on. The circle should enclose the inner bead snugly. Depending on the size of seed beads you use, a circle of six or seven beads may fit better. If your circle seems too big, adapt these instructions to use one or two fewer side beads.

*If you miscalculated and your finished bracelet is too short, a simple trick can make it longer: place **jump rings** between the calotte crimps and the clasp.*

Collar-Net Necklace Project

This necklace looks impressive but isn't technically difficult. It uses netting, a popular off-loom weaving technique which can be worked both vertically and horizontally. This particular pattern is also known as *Greenland Netting*, *Honeycomb Lace*, *Zigzag Lace* and *Mexican Lace*. You'll see this versatile stitch in many different "lace" accessories such as bracelets, collars, hairnets, cuffs and handbags. Often it's directly attached to an object or article of clothing.

The necklace is made by adding three rows of bugle beads and seed beads to a base strand of beads, weaving them horizontally to produce a wonderful effect. Although you can create intricate designs by alternating different colours in a specific pattern, for your first attempt I recommend seed beads and bugle beads of the same colour (see photograph), or at most two contrasting colours. Use beading thread of the same colour as your seed beads to decrease its visibility.

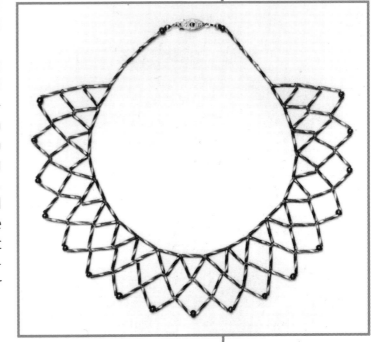

SHOPPING LIST
- 82 size 10° seed beads (or 65 seed beads and 19 pony beads)
- 133—12 mm bugle beads

Note: These quantities yield a 39 cm (15.25 inch) necklace. You may need more or fewer beads if your necklace is a different length or if you use a different size of bugle beads. The finished effect of the net will also be different if you use a different size of bugle beads.

- nylon thread
- 1 clasp
- 2 calotte crimps

TOOL KIT
- beeswax
- beading needle (threader optional)
- scissors
- needle-nose pliers
- tape measure
- adhesive

If you like, substitute pony beads for seed beads in the bottom row, as shown in the photograph, to give the necklace weight. Or use three seed beads instead of one between the bugle beads in the bottom row.

MEASURING YOUR THREAD

This project requires four pieces of thread of varying lengths. First use the measuring tape to determine the length needed for the necklace to rest against the wearer's collarbone. Add 15 cm (6 inches) to the desired length, then double the result and cut your first thread to this length. The remaining three threads should be 20 cm (8 inches) longer than the first. Remember that it's better to have too much thread than too little. The first row uses a doubled thread for added strength (for clarity it's shown as a single thread in the diagram). Place your needle at the centre of the shortest thread so the tails of thread are of equal length. Wax unwaxed thread to prevent knotting.

BEADING

The collar's first-row beads must have holes large enough to take five threads. Also use beads with large holes at the outer edges of rows two and three. Otherwise, if needle and thread can pass through easily, don't worry about hole size.

1. Line up your four threads (the tails of your doubled thread and the three single threads). Pull about 10 cm (4 inches) through the hole in the calotte crimp with the cups facing the short ends of the threads.

2. Pass the short ends through a seed bead small enough to fit inside the calotte crimp. Tie a *granny knot* around the bead about 5 cm (2 inches) from the ends of the threads. Push the calotte crimp up against the knotted bead. See Chapter 10, *Basic Knots,* for instructions on tying granny knots and other knots in this project.

First row

3. Use the needle on the shortest thread to pick up a seed bead and a bugle bead. (If you plan to use pony beads in the bottom row, use a pony bead for the first and last bead in your first row.) Keep alternating seed and bugle beads until you reach a length about 2 cm (3/4 inch) shorter than the planned necklace length. Finish with a seed bead. The calotte crimps and clasp will add the extra length to the necklace.

4. Pass the needle through the hole in the second calotte crimp so the cups face away from the beads.

5. Add a seed bead small enough to fit inside the calotte, push the bead and calotte firmly against the beaded chain and tie an *overhand knot* to secure the thread around the bead. Cut the needle off the thread.

Second row

6. Put the needle on one of the remaining threads and pass the needle through the first 7.6 cm (3 inches) of beads in the first row, emerging after a seed bead.

7. Pick up three beads in this sequence: bugle bead, seed bead, bugle bead. Pass the needle through the next seed bead in the first row and pull the thread tight.

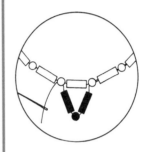

8. Repeat step 7 until you're within 7.6 cm (3 inches) of the end of the first row.

9. Pass the needle through the remaining beads in the first row and then through the hole in the calotte. Knot the thread around the seed bead inside the calotte.

Third row

10. Place the needle on one of the remaining threads, then pass it through the beads in the first row until you reach the place where the second row of beads begins.

11. Pass the needle through the first bugle bead and first seed bead of the second row.

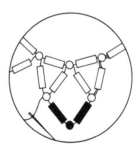

12. Add three beads in this sequence: bugle bead, seed bead, bugle bead. Then pass the needle through the next seed bead in the second row. Pull the thread tight.

13. Repeat step 12 until you have passed the needle through the last seed bead in the second row.

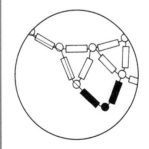

14. Pass the needle through the last bugle bead in the second row, then repeat step 9.

Fourth row

15. Place the needle on the last thread, then pass it through the beads in the first row until you reach the place where the second row begins.

16. Pass the needle through the first bugle bead and first seed bead of the second row, then through the first bugle bead and seed bead of the third row.

17. Pick up three beads in this order: bugle bead, seed bead (or pony bead), bugle bead. Pass the needle through the next seed bead in the third row. Pull the thread tight.

18. Add three beads—bugle bead, seed bead (or pony bead), bugle bead—and pass the needle through the next seed bead in the third row, keeping your thread taut.

19. Repeat step 18 until you have passed the needle through the last seed bead in the third row.

20. Pass the needle through the last bugle bead in the third row and then through the last seed beed and bugle bead in the second row. Repeat step 9.

21. Apply a drop of adhesive to the knotted threads in each calotte crimp.

22. When the adhesive is dry, cut off the excess threads near the knots and close the calotte crimps, using your fingers or pliers. Attach the clasp to the loops in the calotte crimps and close the loops.

Now you've made an easy, beautiful necklace. If you enjoyed this project and you'd like to try other methods, see "Netting Variations" (page 59).

Peyote Bracelet Project

This project introduces one of the most versatile off-loom techniques, the peyote or *gourd stitch*. This stitch was equally popular among early inhabitants of Mesopotamia and native peoples of North America. Both adapted it to a multitude of applications.

The peyote stitch creates a hollow tube of interlocking beads that you can use to surround solid objects of any shape. Native peoples used it to cover talking sticks, peace pipes, containers and other practical and ceremonial objects. Modern beaders have used it to cover purses, hairbands, dog collars, wine bottles and candle holders. But you can also use it to create attractive bracelets and necklaces. This simple stitch is somewhat slower to work than the daisy chain because it uses more beads.

The project shows you how to make the bracelet in the photograph, a simple peyote bracelet with a three-colour candy-stripe design. Choose any three bead colours that strike your fancy and thread to match. For simplicity the instructions refer to the three colours as A, B and C.

SHOPPING LIST
- size 10° seed beads (126 of each colour, plus 2 extra)
  Note: These quantities yield a 17 cm (6.75 inch) bracelet. You may need more or fewer beads if your bracelet is a different length or if you use a different size of seed beads. For example, the first time you try this technique you might find it easier to use larger seed beads, such as size 6°.
- nylon thread
- 1 clasp (choose a type you can fasten with one hand)
- 2 calotte crimps

TOOL KIT
- beeswax
- beading needle (threader optional)
- scissors
- pliers
- tape measure
- adhesive

To help you learn the peyote stitch as quickly as possible, this project gives instructions for three-bead rows. If you'd like to get an even better feel for the peyote stitch, however, and you're willing to invest the extra time, adapt the instructions to make rows of five to seven beads.

MEASURING YOUR THREAD

This technique uses 30 cm (12 inches) of thread for every 2.5 cm (1 inch) of bracelet, so the thread must be twelve times the wearer's wrist measurement. Add 30 cm (12 inches) for finishing. If you run out of thread, or if the thread is too long for comfortable work, add more using the method in Chapter 9, *Solutions to Common Beading Problems*. Wax unwaxed thread to prevent knotting.

BEADING

Make sure the A beads have large holes, because the thread will go through them three times. Also use beads with large holes for the first and last few rows to leave room for the thread that passes through when you attach the calotte crimps.

First row

1. Put a needle on one end of the thread and tie a *slip knot* 7.6 cm (3 inches) from the other end of the thread. (See Chapter 10, *Basic Knots*, for instructions on tying slip knots and other knots used for this project.)

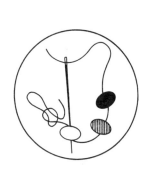

2. Pick up three beads in this sequence: ABC. Push them down the thread to the slip knot, loop the needle through the A bead and pull the thread tight. This completes the first row of your bracelet.

Second row

3. Add one A bead. Pass the needle through the B bead in the first row.

4. Add a B bead and pass the needle through the C bead in the first row.

Try not to insert the needle so that it pierces the threads inside the beads; this will save you time if you have to undo part of the bracelet.

5. Add a C bead and pass the needle through the A bead in the first row, then through the A bead in the second row. Pull the thread tight. This completes your second row.

Third row

6. Add an A bead and pass the needle through the B bead in the previous row.

7. Add a B bead and pass the needle through the C bead in the previous row.

8. Add a C bead and pass the needle through the A bead in the previous row, then through the A bead in the current row. Pull the thread tight. You have now completed three rows and should be well on your way.

Subsequent rows

9. Repeat steps 6 through 8 to add rows until your bracelet reaches the desired length (the wearer's wrist measurement).

ONE-THREAD FINISHING TECHNIQUE

Now you have a piece of peyote-stitch beadwork with a single thread at each end. Add the calotte crimps and clasp with the one-thread finishing technique used for the daisy chain bracelet (page 46).

See "Peyote Variations" (page 60) if you're interested in other ways to use the peyote stitch.

As your tube progresses, it's easy to have a memory lapse and skip a bead colour. I encourage you to undo the work to correct the mistake, because the missing bead throws the whole pattern off.

Off-Loom Weaving

If your bracelet looks like a shapeless pile of beads in which the previous row is indistinguishable from the current row, don't despair. As your tube lengthens, it will shape up until you can easily spot the right bead to thread through. For now, you can tell one row from the other by the number of threads passing through the beads. All the beads in the first row now have two or more threads through them. The current row will have only one thread, except for the A bead which has two. So in step 6 look for the B bead that has a single thread. If you thread through the wrong bead, undo the work back to the error and correct it.

Other Techniques

This section describes variations on techniques used in the three projects, as well as many other off-loom weaving techniques. Some are simple; others are more difficult. Use your imagination to combine techniques and create beadwork of diverse sizes, shapes and patterns.

You've now had practice with bead weaving and can create different effects. The techniques in this section are explained more briefly than the projects, with diagrams to show the movement of the thread.

BRICK STITCH

The brick stitch or *Comanche stitch* creates flat, dense pieces of bead-work in any shape you wish. This stitch is used to form the earring foundation in the fringed earrings project in the *Earrings* chapter.

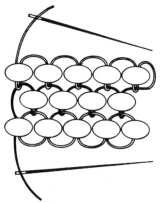

Begin with a foundation row of *two-bead ladder stitch* (see page 57). When you reach the end of the row, pick up a bead with one needle and loop the needle around the thread that's between the last two beads in the foundation row. Then pass the needle back through the bead you just added. Continue adding beads and looping around the thread of the previous row to complete the row and to create additional rows. You can work on one side only of the foundation row or add rows on both sides. To widen the beadwork, pick up two beads at the end of the row. To make it narrower, don't add the last bead in the row.

CHEVRON STITCH

The chevron stitch is very simple, but you can create lots of different chains with it by using different numbers, colours and sizes of beads. Try it with bugle beads too. It gives a zigzag, V or triangle effect, depending on how you vary the bead colours. To start, pick up ten beads, then pass the needle through the first bead again, going in the opposite direction. Add six beads and pass the needle through the eighth bead in the first triangle. Once the second triangle is formed, add six beads at a time and pass the needle through the fourth bead in the previous triangle.

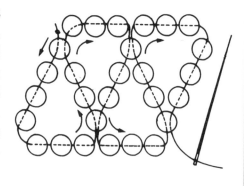

Before you use a new technique, consider whether a single or doubled thread will work best. Take into account how many times the thread passes through the bead holes, the size of the bead holes and the thread thickness. Your goal is always to make your beadwork as secure as possible.

CIRCULAR SHAPES

You can form circular shapes in many ways using off-loom weaving to make pendants, brooches or foundations for earrings. You can also sew them onto clothing or other articles such as purses and belts. The *circular peyote stitch* described under "Peyote Variations" is one way to make circular shapes. Other methods are discussed in the "Advanced Foundations" section of Chapter 2, *Earrings*, and the "Rosettes" section of Chapter 5, *Bead Embroidery*.

As a general rule, to form a circular shape, begin with a single bead, a daisy or a small circle of beads. Add rows of beads around the outside, linking them periodically with the previous inside row, until you reach the desired size. The next two sections describe specific methods for making circular shapes.

Five-triangle circle

Rather than starting in the centre and working outward, this technique involves making five triangles and sewing them together to form a circle. Each triangle combines the *peyote stitch* with the *four-bead ladder stitch*. While fairly complex to construct, the five-triangle circle has a distinctive, solid appearance.

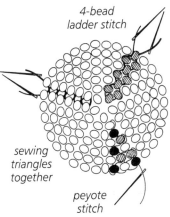

4-bead ladder stitch

sewing triangles together

peyote stitch

To make each triangle, make a foundation row using the four-bead ladder stitch; it should equal the radius (half the width) of the finished circle. Beginning on one side at the bottom of the foundation row, add a bead and pass the needle through the bottom side bead in the foundation row. Use the peyote stitch for flat beadwork to fill in the gaps between the side beads in the foundation row. When the needle is through the last side bead in the foundation row, loop around it and back through the bead you just added. Still using the peyote stitch, work downwards to fill in the gaps in the previous row. When you've passed the needle through the last bead in the previous row, add a bead and then pass the needle through the last bead in the row you just added. Continue to add rows of decreasing length, looping around the top bead in the previous row and adding a bead at the bottom, until the last row is just one bead long. Do the same on the other side of the foundation row to finish the triangle.

When you finish the five triangles, sew them together to form a circle. Fill in the centre of the circle with a bead between each triangle's peak and the next, then put a bead in the very centre. Use **beading graph paper** for the peyote stitch to plan your designs for this technique, as shown in the diagram. Notice that the beads marked with an "X" will be vertical rather than horizontal, since the foundation row uses the four-bead ladder stitch.

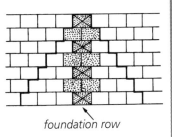

foundation row

Mandala

One way to form a lacy, open circle is by making the mandala shown here, which combines both *netting* and *looping* techniques. You can vary this technique by using different numbers of beads and by altering the number and position of loops.

Begin with a circle of four beads and add a loop of nine beads between each of the first four beads. Pass the needle back through the first loop, emerging after the fifth (outer) bead of the loop. Form a circle by stringing nine beads between the outer beads of each loop.

Create the first loop in the next series of loops by stringing twelve beads and passing through the second nearest bead in the circle. Take the needle back up through the last five beads in the loop you just added. For the remaining loops, pick up seven beads and pass the needle through the second nearest bead in the circle, then back up through the last five beads in the new loop. When you return to the first loop in this layer, add two beads to connect the first and last loops. If you wish, you can add a looped fringe.

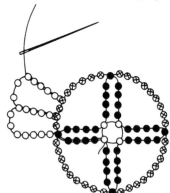

DAISY CHAIN VARIATIONS

The daisy chain you used in the project is called a closed daisy chain. The following techniques are variations on this:

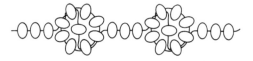

- Create an open daisy chain by stringing on several beads between each daisy.

- Make an overlapping daisy chain by incorporating the last two beads in the previous circle as the first two beads of the current circle.

- Make a doubled daisy chain by beading a second daisy chain next to the first one, using the side beads of the first chain as the side beads in the second chain.

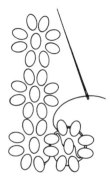

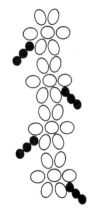

- Add leaves to the completed daisy chain by running the thread back through the chain and adding three beads to each daisy, alternating sides.

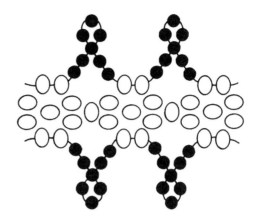

● Make an open daisy chain with one bead between each daisy, then run the thread back along one side to add a loop between each daisy. Then do the other side.

   ● Use the open daisy chain technique, but make a double strand of seed and bugle beads between each daisy.

● Use a larger bead for the centre of the daisy.

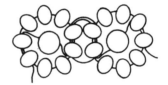

You can also achieve many different effects by changing the colour pattern of the beads. *Zigzag*, *candy-stripe* and *flowers-and-leaves* patterns are just a few of the countless possibilities.

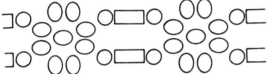

LADDER STITCH AND VARIATIONS

The ladder stitch is a simple technique with many variations. You can use it to create a chain of beads, or you can build a foundation row to use in combination with other techniques. The ladder stitch generally requires two beading needles.

Two-bead ladder stitch

The most basic form of the ladder stitch is used to form the foundation row for the brick stitch and woven earrings (the fringed earrings project

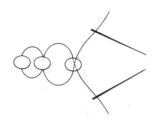

uses a single-needle version of this stitch). It's not often used alone, however, because the thread shows at the sides of the beads. You can use seed beads or bugle beads.

To form a row of beads using the two-bead ladder stitch, put a needle on each end of the thread and position a bead at the middle of the thread. Add a bead with one needle and pass the other needle through this new bead in the opposite direction so the two threads crisscross inside the bead. Pull the thread tight. Continue adding beads until you reach the desired length.

Four-bead ladder stitch

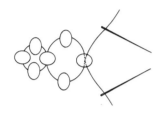

The four-bead ladder stitch can form chains or make foundation rows for other techniques. Form it the same way as the *two-bead ladder stitch*, but pick up a bead with each needle before you add the intersection bead through which both needles pass.

Variations on the ladder stitch

You can alter the ladder stitch slightly by using different types and colours of beads. Other variations include the following:

●Add multiple beads on each side between the intersection beads.

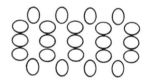

●Use multiple beads for the intersection beads.

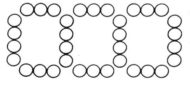

●Use multiple side beads and multiple intersection beads. This creates a chain to wear by itself, as a scarf chain or with a ribbon threaded through it.

●When you reach the end of the row, work backward to add loops to both sides.

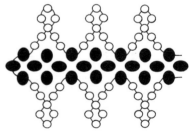

LOOPING STITCH

This is a fun little stitch. A stiff thread or wire will help maintain the loop shapes if you wish. Simply string on ten beads, then loop back through the fifth bead to form the first section. Repeat, adding sections until you reach the desired length. Pull the thread tight; the loops will fall on alternate sides of the central strand to form a wavy line. Feel free to use more or fewer beads in each section and loop.

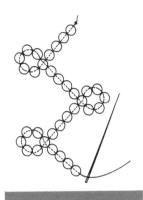

As a general rule, when you add more netting rows, the outer rows should have more beads or larger beads, creating a wider circumference than the inner rows.

NETTING VARIATIONS

The netting technique, also called *latticework* or *lattice stitch*, has many variations. The collar-net necklace project shows you how to work seed beads and bugle beads into a net of four rows using multiple threads. You can also use a single thread, as described in "Single-Thread Netting" (see page 60). Multiple threads offer the advantage of shorter threads which are easier to work with. You can alter the multiple-thread collar netting technique in many ways:

- Instead of using a 7.6 cm (3 inch) lead strand of beads, begin the net right after the calotte crimp.
- Use small bugle beads and only three rows to create a curling effect.
- Add more rows to create a deeper net.
- Add dangles to the centre beads on the bottom row of the net.

The following variations also apply to the single-thread and anchored netting techniques, described later in this section.

- Experiment with bugle beads of different lengths. A 5 mm (1/5 inch) bugle bead will create a much tighter net than a 10 mm (2/5 inch) one.

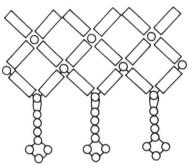

Plan the threads' route before you begin netting. Be sure to use beads with larger holes where the thread will pass through several times.

- Substitute several seed beads for each bugle bead.

- Use larger beads at the intersection points.

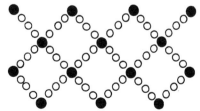

- Use different-coloured beads to create a pattern in the net.

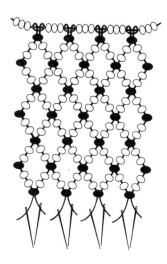

Anchored netting

Anchored netting may be used to create flat or cylindrical shapes. You might use it to attach a net of bugle beads to a favourite vest. This variation employs multiple threads and requires an anchor, such as a string of beads or an edge of cloth or leather, from which the net hangs.

Attach pairs of threads or a double thread to the anchor and work from top to bottom, as shown in the diagram. (Use the *lark's head knot* described in Chapter 10, *Basic Knots,* to anchor doubled threads to a strand of beads.) Adding extra threads at strategic places causes a flat design to fan out or a cylindrical shape to form a cone or bell. You can also widen the design by adding extra beads between the intersection beads as you work downward.

When you've finished beading, use the excess threads to make fringes. On each thread, add enough beads to create your desired fringe length and pass the thread back through all but the last bead. Then weave the thread into the beadwork. If you don't want fringes, just weave the threads back up into the beadwork, knot and clip.

Single-thread netting

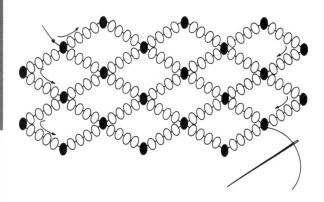

The single-thread netting technique makes beautiful necklaces, as well as flat squares, rectangles, circles or ovals of any size. You can also join the ends of each row to form cylindrical shapes (for example, a beaded cuff or lampshade). To use the single-thread netting technique, simply double back when you reach the end of a row. Make the thread long enough to bead as many rows as you wish, or add new thread when you run out, as described in Chapter 9, *Solutions to Common Beading Problems.*

Bell caps give a neat finish to bracelets and necklaces made using a tube of peyote stitch.

PEYOTE VARIATIONS

The peyote stitch, also called the *gourd stitch*, is one of the most flexible techniques ever invented. It's similar to netting but more closely woven.

The peyote bracelet project demonstrates using the peyote stitch to create a thin, hollow tube. You can also make a wider tube, but a wider hollow tube will collapse and lie flat (which may be what you want). You can also bead around cords. The peyote stitch will cover an object of any shape: spherical, rectangular or graduated in size. It will also produce flat beadwork.

One-drop peyote stitch

This section describes how to use the one-drop peyote stitch to create flat beadwork, and to bead around objects.

Flat beadwork. Begin by stringing on enough beads to reach the desired width for the beadwork, using an even number of beads. These beads form the base row, which is actually the first two rows of the beadwork. To begin the next row, add a bead and pass the needle back through the second-to-last bead in the base row. Pull the thread tight so the beads shift into a bricklike position. Add another bead and pass the needle through the fourth-to-last bead in the base row. Continue adding beads and passing the needle through every second bead in the base row until you've passed the needle through the first bead in the base row.

Now you've completed the third row, which has half the number of beads as the base row. Add a bead and pass the needle through the last bead in the third row. Continue along the width of the beadwork, adding a bead between each bead in the previous row. Consult the diagram if you're not sure what to do at the end of the row.

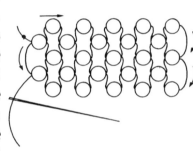

Tapering flat beadwork. To taper your flat peyote stitch beadwork so it becomes narrower, don't add the first bead in the new row; instead, pass the needle back into the last bead you added. Do the same when you reach the end of the row and begin the next one so the beadwork tapers evenly on both sides. The beadwork will now be two beads narrower. Continue to skip the first bead of each new row until you've reached the desired width. If you want the beadwork to taper gradually, bead a few rows at the new width before dropping more beads.

The easiest way to taper peyote stitch beadwork so it becomes wider is to bead the widest part first, then use the technique for narrowing the beadwork, described in the previous paragraph. So if you want an egg-shaped piece of flat beadwork, widest at the middle and narrower toward each

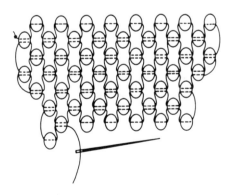

Off-Loom Weaving

end, bead the wide section first, then taper the nearest end, then begin at the other side of the wide section to taper that end.

Another, more difficult, method to make the beadwork wider is to add two beads instead of one when you begin a new row. Do the same when you begin the next row so the beadwork tapers evenly on both sides. The beadwork will now be two beads wider. Continue to add an extra bead at the beginning of each row until you reach the desired width. If you want the beadwork to taper gradually, bead a few rows at the new width before adding more beads.

Beading around objects. To use the one-drop peyote stitch to bead around objects, make your base row as long as needed to go around the object, using an even number of beads. Pass the needle through the first bead again, add a bead and pass the needle through the third bead in the base row. Continue adding beads and passing your needle through every second bead in the base row. Pull the thread tight so the beads shift into a bricklike position. Pass the needle through the first bead in the row you just added before beginning the next row.

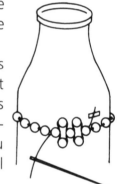

You may want to bead the first few rows before you anchor the beadwork to the object (but check frequently to ensure your beadwork fits snugly around the object). To anchor your bead-work, tape the thread tail to the object. When you finish beading, remove the tape and weave the tail into the beadwork.

Tapering three-dimensional beadwork. As with flat bead-work, the easiest way to taper the peyote stitch as you're beading around an object is to begin with the widest section, then narrow the beadwork. For example, if you're covering a wine bottle, bead the widest part first, then taper the beadwork (as described next) to cover the bottom and the neck.

Tapering three-dimensional beadwork is a little more compli-cated than flat beadwork, because you must skip beads regularly around the circumference of the object for the tapering to be even. For example, if your current row is 28 beads long, and the next row should have 21 beads, you need to skip one out of every four beads. To skip a bead, just pass the needle through the next bead in the previous row without adding a bead, as shown in the diagram (the space

When tapering three-dimensional beadwork, *to calculate the number of beads needed for the next row, string on some loose beads and drape the strand where the next row will go, adding more beads if the strand isn't long enough. Count the beads on the strand, and divide this number by two (because the second row will fill the gaps left by the beads in the row you add next). Remove the beads before you continue, then bead the next two rows using the number of beads you calculated. After you do this a few times you'll probably be able to judge where to skip a bead simply by looking at the beadwork.*

between the beads is exaggerated to show the movement of the thread).

To make the beadwork wider (if you decide against beading the widest part first and then narrowing the beadwork), add extra beads when you reach the place where the object widens. Calculate the number of beads needed for the next row, and space the extra beads evenly throughout the row. To add an extra bead, pick up two beads instead of one, then pass the needle through the next bead in the previous row.

Two-drop peyote stitch

In the two-drop peyote stitch, use two beads at a time instead of one, following the same method as in the *one-drop peyote stitch*.

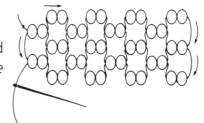

Circular peyote stitch

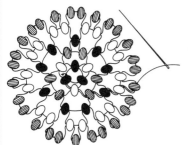

You can also use the peyote stitch to make flat, circular shapes. One way is to begin with a small inner circle of three to five beads, then add two beads at a time for the next circle, one bead at a time for the third circle, two beads at a time for the fourth circle and so on. Note that this two-bead, one-bead pattern is a suggestion only; the size and shape of the beads you're using will dictate how to place them.

RIGHT-ANGLE WEAVE

In the right-angle weave, the beads in one row are at right angles to those in the next row. Right-angle weaving works well to make square or rectangular shapes.

One way to form the right-angle weave re-quires multiple threads and combines aspects of the *anchored netting* technique and the *four-bead ladder stitch*. Anchor pairs of threads or doubled threads and work from top to bottom. For the first row, add a bead to each of the two outer threads and to the pairs of threads between them. For the second row, beginning with the two left-hand threads, pass both threads through another bead so the threads crisscross inside the bead. Repeat for each pair of threads. Alternate the first and second rows' methods to add more rows. You can make fringes with the excess thread if you wish.

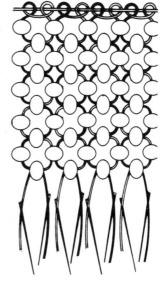

SQUARE STITCH

The square stitch, which resembles loom woven beadwork, can be used to create flat squares or rectangles. As with any flat shape, you can turn it into a cylinder by sewing the edges together once you finish. String as many beads as needed to reach the desired length for the first row. Add two beads and loop through the second-to-last bead in the first row, then through the last bead you added. Pick up a bead and loop through the third-to-last bead in the previous row, then through the bead you just added. Continue adding beads and looping through the beads of the previous row.

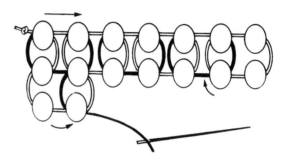

Finishing Techniques

Finishing a piece of beadwork can be as simple as knotting the ends of a long chain together or as complicated as melting gold to cast your own jewellery findings. The most important goal of any finishing technique is to secure the thread so the beadwork doesn't come undone. Another important aspect is to neatly conceal the threads and knots. Finishing techniques can also give your beadwork flexibility, allowing you to put the beadwork on and take it off again. If you're making a bracelet, remember to choose a clasp that you can fasten with one hand!

This section describes finishing techniques that give your beadwork a professional finish. Some incorporate the jewellery findings listed in Chapter 11, *Tools and Materials*. Also see the "Finishing Techniques" sections in Chapter 1, *Stringing*, and Chapter 4, *Loom Weaving*, for additional ideas about how to finish your off-loom woven beadwork.

You can plan your finishing technique before you begin beading and incorporate it into your beadwork, as in the collar-net necklace project, or you can apply the finishing technique after you complete the beadwork. Either way, always allow enough thread for finishing. You'll find 15 cm (6 inches) of thread at each end adequate for most finishing techniques.

ONE-THREAD FINISHING

The one-thread finishing technique, described in the daisy chain bracelet project instructions, can be used for any off-loom woven beadwork that results in one thread at either end.

To use this technique, add a **calotte crimp** and a seed bead small enough to fit inside it. Weave back through a few beads in the beadwork, then circle back through the calotte crimp, bead and beadwork again. Finish by knotting the thread around the bead in the calotte crimp. Add a small drop of adhesive to the knot; when it's dry, cut off excess thread, close the calotte crimp and attach the clasp.

The bead anchors the knot inside the calotte crimp; otherwise it's hard to make a knot in a single thread large enough to prevent it from slipping through the calotte crimp hole. Weaving through the beadwork, calotte and bead several times strengthens the closure, which is typically the weakest spot in a piece of jewellery. If you can't weave through the beadwork because it ends with a strand of beads (as with the *looping stitch*), use a single strand finishing technique from Chapter 1, *Stringing*.

TWO-THREAD FINISHING

If you have two threads at each end of the beadwork, you can adapt the one-thread finishing technique.

Pass both threads through the hole in a calotte crimp, put a small seed bead on one of the threads, then knot the threads together. You don't need to weave back through the beadwork, but you miss out on the strengthening benefit if you don't.

If you use a technique such as the *ladder stitch*, you end up with two threads at one end and no threads at the other end. You can either use a new thread to attach a calotte crimp and small seed bead to the beadwork, weaving through about 1.3 cm (1/2 inch) of beadwork to secure the thread. Or you can plan for this by passing the thread through a small seed bead and calotte crimp before you begin beading.

MULTIPLE-THREAD FINISHING
Use this technique if you have more than two threads at the ends of your beadwork.

Pass all the threads through the hole in a calotte crimp. Knot the threads together. Apply a drop of adhesive to the knot. When the adhesive has dried, cut off excess thread, close the calotte crimp and attach the clasp.

You can use a small seed bead inside the calotte, though it's not necessary. The collar-net necklace project, for example, uses a seed bead to anchor the threads one at a time as the beadwork progresses.

Chapter 1, *Stringing*, discusses other methods of multiple-strand finishing.

FINISHING WIDER OFF-LOOM WOVEN BEADWORK
Many techniques in this chapter can create wide or large pieces of beadwork. It's most important to secure the thread so the beadwork won't come undone.

Additional finishing elements depend on how you want to use the pieces. You can attach a chain of beads to make a pendant, attach fringes around the edges, sew beadwork onto clothing or belts, attach a beaded cord to make wall hangings or leave the beadwork as a freestanding or flat-lying piece. The "Finishing Techniques" section in Chapter 4, *Loom Weaving*, provides ideas that are equally suitable for wide off-loom work. Chapter 6, *Other Things You Can Bead*, describes how to make off-loom woven beadwork into hangings.

To secure the threads of off-loom woven beadwork, simply weave the ends back into the beadwork. Then knot the thread tail around a thread in the beadwork, run the tail through a few more beads and cut off excess thread. For extra security, you may prefer to knot the thread tail again and run it through a few more beads before cutting off the excess.

The loops on clasps should be aligned so the ends join to form a closed loop. Bend the wire with pliers to close gaps.

Apply a small drop of adhesive to the join of clasp loops and jump rings after you attach them to your beadwork.

Chapter Four
Loom Weaving

Loom weaving is simple to do, but you can use it to create varied and complex beadwork. And nothing is more thrilling than planning a design on graph paper and seeing it take shape on the loom. You can translate almost any image into beaded loom work: your own doodles or sketches, photographs or drawings you find in books, flowers, landscapes, random slashes of colour and geometric designs.

But the versatility of beaded loom work doesn't end with design; you can also put the finished work to many uses. The wonderfully textured beaded fabric makes great bracelets, wristbands, barrettes, necklaces, chokers, headbands, hatbands, belts, mats and hangings. You can sew completed loom work onto clothing to make a beaded collar or neckline for a blouse, or to trim pockets, hems and cuffs. Combine fringes with loom woven beadwork and you have an object of true beauty.

This chapter begins with a simple loom weaving project to help you learn the basics. The second section discusses different looms and offers working tips for loom woven beadwork. The third describes variations on the basic loom weaving technique. The final section gives other techniques for finishing the work once it's off the loom. Finishing the warp threads neatly is one of the biggest challenges of loom work.

Loom Woven Bracelet Project

As you do this introductory project, you'll see how simply this technique lends itself to creating patterns through colour. You may also be surprised by how easy it is to do loom weaving. The texture of loom woven beadwork is so appealing that you'll probably want to use this pliable, beaded fabric to create many new wardrobe accessories.

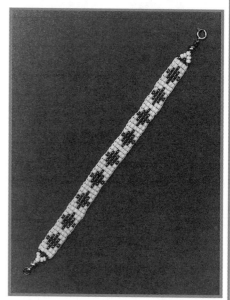

The project includes a simple pattern that shouldn't distract you from the beading process. The technique itself is so straightforward, however, that you'll soon get the hang of it. Then you'll be free to experiment with more difficult patterns, and even better, create your own. In this project you'll weave a bracelet five beads wide with a simple geometric design in three colours.

The bracelet in the photograph uses purple and red beads on a white background (and extra-thick thread for illustrative purposes), but choose any colours you like. Try to use beading thread that matches the beads that form the bracelet's background. The instructions refer to the colours as A, B and C.

SHOPPING LIST

- size 10^{0} seed beads (170 colour A, 78 colour B, 47 colour C)
  Note: These quantities yield a 17 cm (6.75 inch) bracelet. You may need more or fewer beads if your bracelet is a different length or if you use a different size of seed beads.
- nylon thread
- 1 clasp (choose a type that you can fasten with one hand)
- 2 calotte crimps

TOOL KIT

- bead loom
- beeswax
- beading needle (threader optional)
- scissors
- needle-nose pliers
- tape measure
- adhesive

MEASURING YOUR THREAD

This project gives instructions for using a commercially available wire and wood dowel loom. You may need to use a different method to attach the warp threads if you use a different type of loom.

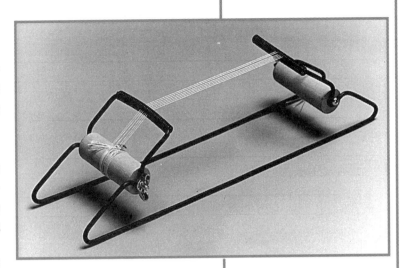

1. Warp threads attach to the loom and run lengthwise through the bracelet. There is always one more warp thread than the number of beads across your beadwork.

Decide on the bracelet's finished length. Its loom woven portion should be 2.5 cm (1 inch) shorter than the wearer's wrist measurement. Add 30 cm (12 inches) to this measurement and cut six threads of this length. Wax the six threads if they're unwaxed (to strengthen them and protect them from moisture) and knot them together about 2.5 cm (1 inch) from the end. Attach them to one end of the loom. Position the threads between the grooves at each end of the loom. Knot the free ends of thread together about 2.5 cm (1 inch) from the end and attach them to the other end of the loom. Wind any excess thread around the dowel.

Use a needle to separate the threads and position them between the grooves.

2. Weft threads go across the width of the beadwork, perpendicular to the warp threads, and anchor the beads in place.

Multiply the desired length of the beadwork by nine and add 30 cm (12 inches); cut your weft thread to this length. (Note that this project gives instructions for using a single thread; if you were using a doubled thread you would double the length.) If it turns out to be too short or you can't work comfortably with this much thread, see Chapter 9, *Solutions to Common Beading Problems*, for instructions on adding thread. Wax unwaxed thread to prevent knotting.

If you have difficulty attaching the warp threads to the loom, read your loom's instructions.

BEADING

Use beads that are consistent in size (both length and diameter) to achieve an even width for your bracelet.

1. Thread a needle onto your weft thread. The first row begins about 13 cm (5 inches) from where the warp threads are attached to the loom. You can knot the weft thread to the outer warp thread where the first row begins, if you like, leaving a 15 cm (6 inch) tail.

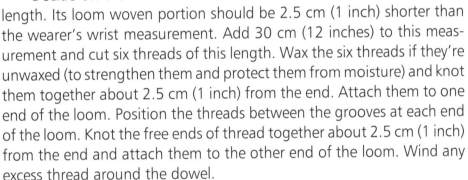

Loom Weaving

2. Pick up five A beads and push them 15 cm (6 inches) from the end of the weft thread (or against the knot, if you've used one). Pass the needle under the loom. Push the beads up between the warp threads, holding them in position with one forefinger.

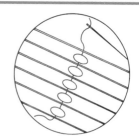

3. Push the needle back through the beads, this time above the warp threads, to anchor the first row in position. Look for the silver glint of the needle as it passes over the threads, making sure you don't pierce a warp thread as the needle passes over them.

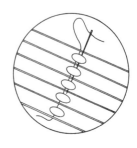

On a commercial wire-and-dowel loom, when you run out of working room, wind the completed beadwork onto the first dowel, exposing more warp thread.

4. Pick up 5 beads in this order: AABAA.

5. Push these beads up between the warp threads and again pass the needle back through the beads but above the warp threads.

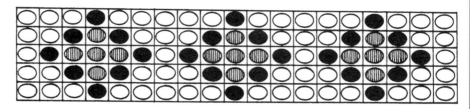

6. Repeat steps 4 and 5, following the pattern to add five beads each time, until you have reached the desired length.

Try to finish the beadwork at the end of the pattern sequence with a row of A beads. If necessary you can make the woven part as much as 1.3 cm (1/2 inch) shorter, or a bit longer, than you planned.

7. After you complete the last row of beads, pass the needle and thread back through 2.5 cm to 5 cm (1 inch to 2 inches) of the previous rows. Knot the thread around the weft thread, then pass the needle through a few more beads. Cut the thread close to the beadwork. (Cut it between two beads, not at the end of a row where the tip may show.)

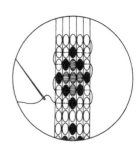

8. Repeat step 7 with the tail of thread at the beginning of the beadwork.

9. Remove the beadwork from the loom. Untie or cut off the knots in the warp threads.

TAPERED BEADED FINISHING TECHNIQUE

Now you have a piece of loom woven beadwork with six warp threads at each end. It's time to finish the warp threads and add the calotte crimps and clasp.

1. Divide the warp threads at one end of the beadwork into three pairs.

2. Add a C bead and then an A bead to the two outer pairs of thread, and a B bead and then a C bead to the middle pair of threads. Push the beads up tightly against the beadwork.

3. Gather the warp threads into two groups of three threads and string an A bead on each group.

4. Pass all six warp threads through an A bead, then through the hole in a calotte crimp; the cups should face away from the beadwork.

5. Knot the threads around a needle, using an *overhand knot* (if necessary see Chapter 10, *Basic Knots*), as close to the calotte crimp as possible. Use the needle to slide the knot into the crimp.

6. Repeat steps 1 through 5 for the warp threads at the other end of the beadwork.

7. Apply a drop of adhesive to the knotted threads in the crimps at each end of the bracelet. When the adhesive is dry, cut off excess threads close to the knots.

8. Close the calotte crimps with your fingers or pliers. Attach the clasp to the loops in the calotte crimps and close the loops.

Now you know how to use a bead loom and you have a new bracelet. See the next section, "Getting Started in Loom Weaving," for more information about loom weaving.

If you miscalculated and your finished bracelet is too short, a simple trick can make it longer: place **jump rings** between the calotte crimps and the clasp.

Loom Weaving

Getting Started in Loom Weaving

This chapter's bracelet project shows you the basic techniques for loom weaving. This section describes different kinds of looms you can use and offers general tips for any loom weaving project.

LOOMS

Traditionally, beaders have used many kinds of looms to create beaded loom work. The basic wire-and-dowel loom available in most bead stores and hobby shops can meet your basic looming needs, but it does have limitations. The width of beadwork prepared on this type of loom is restricted to the number of grooves (about thirty) in the spring-coil at each end. Also, the working area is quite short. While you can wind completed sections onto the first dowel to make more room to work, you can't see the entire piece of beadwork at once. This also makes it harder to measure the length of completed beadwork.

warp threads

strip of suede

small hook

If you want to make a wider piece using a wire-and-dowel loom, first make separate narrow pieces. Sew them together by weaving your needle and thread through the outer three or four beads in each row of the two pieces of beadwork. Another option is to make your own custom-designed loom to accommodate the size of your bead-work.

A custom-designed loom is easy to construct and can be made from many different materials, as long as they're strong enough to maintain even tension in the warp threads. You can use carved grooves to hold the warp threads in position (fasten the threads to a nail or hook) or pound in nails to wind the threads around. If you choose to string your loom by winding your threads around nails, make sure the loom is long enough to hold your beadwork plus extra thread at each end for your finishing technique.

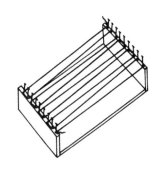

Attach a piece of suede to each end of a wooden loom, between the grooves and the hook or nail, to prevent the warp threads from slipping or fraying.

GENERAL LOOM WEAVING TIPS

- Always choose a finishing technique before you prepare warp threads so that you allow enough thread.
- For best results keep your warp threads taut; make sure the tension is equal for all warp threads.
- Consider whether a single or doubled weft thread will work best for your project. If you're using beads with large holes and want

Loom Weaving

to make your beadwork extra strong, it's a good idea to double the thread. Just remember that when you add a new thread and weave in thread tails, all of those threads also have to fit through the holes in the beads. On the other hand, a single thread is usually strong enough and is easier to work with. Try both methods to see which you prefer.

● To calculate the length of a single weft thread, multiply the length of each row by the number of rows, double this amount and add 15 cm to 30 cm (6 inches to 12 inches) at each end for weaving in the tails of the threads (multiply this amount by two if you're using a doubled weft thread). Of course, if you're making a large piece of beadwork, it's impossible to do the whole thing with one piece of thread. In this case use a length you're comfortable with and add more when you run out, as described in Chapter 9, *Solutions to Common Beading Problems*.

● Once you finish adding rows to your loom work, weave your weft thread through the last four rows. Knot it around the weft thread between two beads using an *overhand knot*, and weave through a few more beads before cutting off the tail. (Cut off the tail between two beads rather than at the end of the row so it won't show.) Repeat for the tail of weft thread at the beginning of your loom work.

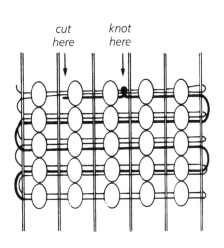

cut here   knot here

Once you finish *beading, you may notice that in some areas the weft thread doesn't go both under and over the warp threads, causing the warp threads to float above the surface of the beads. If this happens, correct the problem by taking a new thread and weaving through the beads again, both under and over the warp threads of the affected rows.*

● Use **beading graph paper** to plan your designs. See Chapter 8, *Planning and Design*, for information and ideas. If your design is complex, try putting the graph paper directly beneath the threads on your loom. You can easily see it and make sure your beadwork is accurate.

● Double the warp threads on the outer edges of your beadwork, if you like, for added strength.

● For loom woven beadwork, you should generally use beads that are consistent in size to achieve a uniform width and surface, but don't be afraid to experiment and have fun. If you don't like the results of your experiment, you can always start over again.

Loom Weaving

Other Techniques

This section shows you some variations on the basic loom weaving technique.

BEADED WARP TECHNIQUE

Use this method to string sections of beads between solidly woven sections. String the desired number of beads onto the warp threads before attaching threads to the loom. Keep the beads at the unworked end of the loom, then move them into position when you reach the place where you want the beaded warps to begin. Use a strong thread for your warps so the unwoven warp threads don't break.

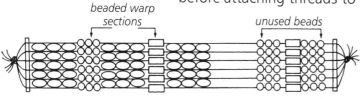

beaded warp
sections

unused beads

SPLIT LOOM WORK

Use this method to create splits in your loom work or to produce loom woven fringes at the ends of the beadwork.

To illustrate, say you want a split that's one bead wide in the centre of a piece that's five beads wide. When you reach the place where you want the split to begin, bead rows that are two beads wide for the length of the split. To fill in the beadwork on the other side of the split, work the thread back to where the split began or use a new thread. Pass the thread through the last full row, then bead rows that are two beads wide for the full length of the split. When you reach the end of the split, resume beading rows across the full width of the beadwork. It's a good idea to reinforce the beadwork at both ends of the split: connect the full rows to the first and last split rows by passing the needle through the beads at the rows' outer edges and the beads closest to the split.

If you want the two sections to touch each other without a

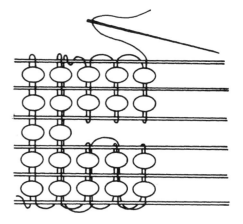

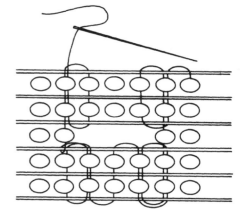

one-bead-wide gap, as you may for split fringes, use a double warp thread. This requires planning ahead! Take care to pass the weft thread at the end of the row on one side of the split around one warp thread only. Anchor the rows on the other side of the split to the other warp thread. If you're making split loom work fringes at the end of the beadwork, note that they won't actually spread out until you remove the beadwork from the loom.

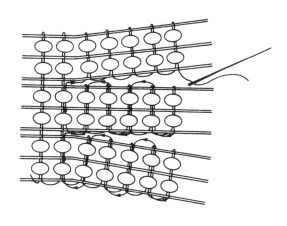

TAPERING LOOM WORK

To taper your loom work, after you make the last full row of beads add a row two beads shorter (one bead shorter on each side). To begin a shorter row, pass the needle back through the first seed bead in the previous row, underneath the first and second warp threads. Pull the needle up between the second warp thread and the second bead, then pass it back around and under the second warp thread. Add the beads for the next row and press the beads up between the warp threads as usual. Continue adding shorter rows of beads until the last row is just one or two beads long. Use the clean-edge finish described in the "Finishing Techniques" section to weave in the warp threads, or add end fringes (described in the same section).

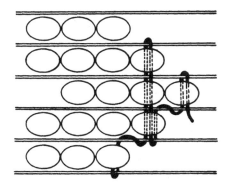

Finishing Techniques

The main challenge of loom woven beadwork, aside from the design, is what to do with the warp threads once you've finished beading. The techniques in this section illustrate different ways to make a neat, stable finish. Unless otherwise stated, each finishing technique requires that the warp threads extend beyond the beadwork about 15 cm (6 inches) at each end.

USING CRIMPS, CLASPS AND END SPACERS

If your loom work is narrow you can use a simple crimp and clasp finish. Once it's more than a few beads wide, though, the outside threads will be too long between the beadwork and the crimp, and will cause the beadwork to curl at the edges. Another potential problem is that the exposed warp threads may fray or catch on something sharp and break. See "Tapered Beaded Finish," next, for an attractive alternative.

If your beadwork is so wide that all of its threads won't fit through a single calotte crimp's hole, try using multiple crimps and attaching them to an end spacer. You can attach the beadwork directly to the calotte crimps or use a multi-tapered beaded finish before attaching the calotte crimps.

TAPERED BEADED FINISH

You can protect and conceal the threads with the tapered beaded finishing technique described in this chapter's beginning project. Use your imagination to incorporate the design of the beadwork into the finishing beads. Begin by adding a bead or two to each warp thread, or to pairs of warp threads. Continue to consolidate the threads into ever larger groups as you extend the taper.

CLEAN-EDGE FINISH

The clean-edge finish, developed by Jacqui Bellefontaine, a beader from British Columbia, allows you to secure the warp threads to beaded loom work in a seemingly invisible fashion. (It is most invisible when your warp threads are fine.) This technique employs the whip stitch (a series of *half-hitches*) to wrap each warp thread around itself, holding the beads in position. Use the finish before attaching the loom work to cloth, leather or a garment. It's also useful for freestanding pieces such as mats with or without a fringe. The next two sections provide information about end fringes and side fringes.

To give your beadwork a clean-edge finish, weave in the tails of the weft thread as described in "General Loom Weaving Tips" on page 72. Remove your beadwork from the loom and put a needle on one end of the first warp thread. Bring the needle up through the beadwork, along the inner edge of the warp thread, between the first and second rows of beads. Pull the thread snug but not tight enough to pucker the beadwork. Then bring the needle up between the second and third rows of beads. Continue with the whip stitch for several more rows.

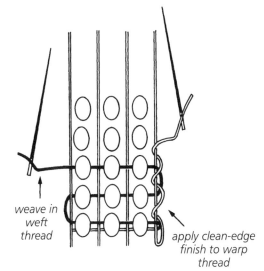

weave in weft thread

apply clean-edge finish to warp thread

Cut off excess thread. Or, if you're using a slippery thread, to prevent it from coming undone, weave the thread through several beads before cutting off excess thread; I prefer this method, especially for the outer warp threads, but it does mean wrapping the warp threads for consecutively longer distances to avoid weaving through the same beads. (If using this method, be sure to cut excess threads between two beads, not at the end of the row.) Repeat for the other outer warp thread, then do the inner warp threads. Repeat for the other end of the loom work. This is time-consuming, but your loom work will have a neat, secure finish.

You can also adapt the clean-edge finish to make continuous pieces of beaded loom work such as rings, headbands and long necklaces. Simply wrap the warp threads around the warp threads at the other end of the beadwork for 2.5 cm to 5 cm (1 inch to 2 inches). Once you've woven in the warp threads, weave the weft threads on either side of the join into the loom work on the opposite side of the join.

END FRINGES

Beaded loom work looks especially beautiful when you turn the warp threads at each end into beaded fringes. Allow for this when you prepare the threads. Decide how long you want the fringe to be; calculate the longest part if you plan tapered fringes. Double the length of the longest fringe (quadruple it if you plan to have fringes at both ends) and add 30 cm (12 inches) for finishing.

Before adding fringe beads, design the fringe on **beading graph paper** for loom work. Combine seed beads with bugle beads or larger beads if you wish. You can order the seed beads to repeat your loom work's pattern or even arrange them to form letters and words. For more ideas, see the "Fringed Earring Variations" section in the *Earrings* chapter.

Before you make the fringes, weave in the tails of the weft thread as described in "General Loom Weaving Tips" on page 72.

Remove your beadwork from the loom and put a needle on the first warp thread at one end. Add beads according to your design and push them up snugly against the loom work. Pass the needle back through all but the bottom bead, or if your fringe ends in a loop, the bottom bead group. Hold the bottom bead and pull the thread firmly through the top bead in the fringe; the fringe should hang naturally with no thread showing.

Then apply the clean-edge finish to secure the warp thread. Do the same for the remaining warp threads. For tapered fringes, adjust the fringe design as you bead if the taper develops too sharply or too gradually. Repeat to finish the other end of the loom work, or use a different finish.

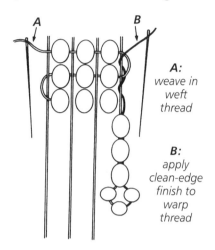

A: weave in weft thread

B: apply clean-edge finish to warp thread

Another method for making end fringes is to make split loom work fringes using doubled warp threads, as described in the "Other Techniques" section.

SIDE FRINGES

Side fringes, either in addition to or instead of end fringes, also add an attractive dimension to your loom work. They're best attached after you've removed your beadwork from the loom and woven in the warp threads for a clean-edge finish.

Begin by knotting your waxed thread between two beads in the fourth row. Put a needle on your thread and weave from the fourth to the first row, emerging from the first row on the side where you want the fringe. Add the fringe as you would an end fringe. Pass the needle back up through the first row of the loom work, then down through the next row. Repeat until you've added all the fringes, then weave the thread through the first four rows of loom work at the other end and knot it between two beads. Weave both ends of the thread through a few more beads, then cut them off close to the bead-work.

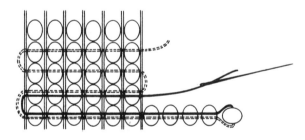

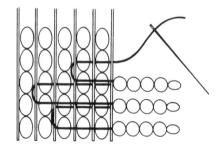

Plan your side fringe design as you would for an end fringe. To determine the amount of thread needed, add the length of the longest fringe to the width of the beadwork. Multiply by two. Then multiply this amount by the number of fringes and add 30 cm (12 inches).

If your loom work is too wide to run the fringe thread from one side to the other, pass the thread through a few beads in each row. Alter the number of beads each time so the fringe's weight doesn't all rest on one warp thread.

WALL HANGINGS

You can make narrow or wide pieces of loom woven beadwork into hangings. See Chapter 6, *Other Things You Can Bead,* for information.

SEWING ONTO CLOTH OR LEATHER

You can use this method to sew beadwork onto a garment, or to attach a reinforcing backing to beadwork to be worn alone. To make a beaded belt, use this method to sew your beadwork onto an old belt. You can also use it to back off-loom and loom woven beadwork that you want to fasten to a ring, barrette or brooch finding.

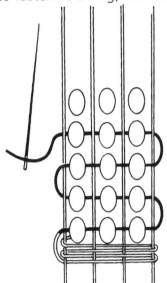

For loom woven beadwork, before you remove the work from the loom, weave the weft thread alone (without beads) over and under your warp threads for a few rows, then weave it into the beadwork. Do this at both ends of the beadwork, to prevent the beads in the first and last rows from sliding out of position. Remove the work from the loom and apply the clean-edge finish. If you don't want to use the clean-edge finish, trim the warp threads to a length of 2.5 to 5 cm (1 to 2 inches), and fasten them underneath the beadwork using basting tape (available at sewing shops).

Use a beading needle for the sewing; it's thin enough to pass through most materials easily. If you are sewing onto thick leather, however, you may need an **awl** to punch holes first. Plan where you want the holes before you punch. Or use a special **glover needle** designed to slide easily through leather.

First place the beadwork in position; hold it with pins or tape if you wish. For loom work, tuck the rows of unbeaded weft threads underneath. Sew on the beadwork with a needle and thread by passing the needle between the outer warp threads and the beadwork and then through the cloth. (For off-loom woven beadwork, stitch down the threads that run through the beads at the outer edges.) Stitch between each outer bead, sewing around each side and end of the beadwork (at the ends of loom work, stitch down the weft thread in the final row of beads).

If you want to attach your beadwork to a barrette, screened disk or other finding, see Chapter 6, *Other Things You Can Bead.*

Place knots *between the beadwork and the cloth. (Knots on the back of the cloth tend to come undone as the cloth rubs against your skin.) One way of securing the thread tail is to sew several tiny stitches on top of each other.*

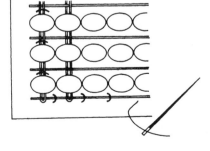

Loom Weaving

CLOTH FASTENERS

Another way to finish a wide piece of loom work that you want to put on and take off, such as a choker or wristband, is to make cloth fasteners. You can use them for loom work with end fringes or a clean-edge finish. Any nonstretchable fabric will do; velvet is especially attractive.

If you've left a gap where the two ends of the beadwork join together, make the fasteners the same width as the beadwork and long enough to fill the gap between the ends of beadwork. Allow a small overlap for **sewing snaps** or **hooks and eyes**. Attach the beadwork to the fasteners, then check the fit to line up the fasteners before sewing on the snaps or hooks and eyes. Use as many snaps or hooks and eyes as needed to hold the two fasteners together securely. If you like, decorate the outer side of the cloth fastener with beads that match the loom work (see Chapter 5, *Bead Embroidery*, for more information about making beaded designs on cloth).

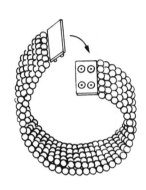

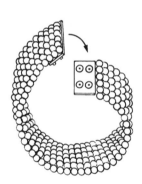

As an alternative to this finishing technique, fully back the beadwork with cloth or leather. Add snaps or hooks and eyes to hold the overlapping ends of the backing shut.

If one end of the beadwork meets flush with the other end, sew one side of the fastener on the underside of the beadwork, as shown in the diagram. See "Sewing onto Cloth or Leather" earlier in this chapter for more information.

Loom Weaving

Chapter Five
Bead Embroidery

Embroidering beads onto clothing or other fabric or leather objects is a time-honoured craft.

Bead embroidery can enhance and embellish clothing to create effects ranging from counter-culture to haute couture. It can adorn the bodices and yokes of dresses, skirts and blouses, as well as waistband areas, collars and cuffs, sleeves and pockets. It can decorate vests, T-shirts, jackets, cloaks, pants, belts, hats, gloves, scarves, shoes, bags, tapestries, cushions . . . in fact, almost anything you can imagine.

Seed beads, bugle beads and larger beads can be used to create embroidered designs, edgings and fringes.

You can embroider directly onto a garment or other article, or you can embroider onto a piece of cloth which you then sew on to the article. The latter method is called *appliqué,* from the French word meaning to apply or put on.

This chapter begins with a bead embroidery project to let you try some basic embroidery stitches. The second section discusses special materials needed for bead embroidery. The third section describes several methods for preparing a design and applying it to the fabric. The last part of the chapter illustrates basic bead embroidery stitches.

Bead Embroidery Sampler

Before you begin embroidering beads directly onto your clothes, try this project. It gives you a feel for attaching beads to cloth as well as practice with some basic stitches. It also gives practice in transferring a pattern onto fabric.

The project shows you how to create a geometric, stylized flower-and-leaves design. This design is a simplified version of a pattern used by the Nez Perce people around 1890. You can embroider it using a framing hoop, which allows you to hang it without transferring it into another frame. Or you can sew the finished bead embroidery onto a jean jacket, T-shirt, bag or cushion.

If you plan to attach the beadwork to a piece of clothing, you might want to try this project without a hoop, as the bead rows may pucker when released from the tension of a hoop. While it seems more difficult at first, with a little experience it is actually easier to manipulate the fabric as you embroider when you don't use a hoop. You'll learn with practice to bead with the correct tension. On the other hand, you might as well use a hoop if you plan to use your embroidery as a picture, so it will be framed and ready to hang.

SHOPPING LIST
- 15 cm (6 inch) circular framing hoop or regular embroidery hoop
- 20 cm by 20 cm (8 inch by 8 inch) piece of chamois or heavy cloth (denim if the piece is intended for your jean jacket, or inexpensive heavy canvas)
- size 10° seed beads in five colours:
  85 colour A
  628 colour B
  492 colour C
  608 colour D
  368 colour E
  Note: The quantities given are approximate and may vary slightly from beader to beader. You will need fewer beads if you use a larger bead size.
- thread to match your cloth
- tracing paper
- light blue tailor's chalk

TOOL KIT
- beading needle (threader optional)
- beeswax
- scissors
- regular pencil (use a pencil with a soft lead, such as a #2)

The instructions for this project are for size 10° seed beads, but feel free to substitute larger beads such as 8° or 6°. The results won't be as neat, but you'll be able to form and fill the guidelines with fewer beads, thus completing the project more quickly.

PREPARING THE FABRIC

Begin by preparing a pattern to follow. The pattern in this book is to scale (the actual finished size). If you wish to alter the size, use a photocopy machine to reduce or enlarge it.

1. Place your tracing paper over the pattern below. Draw the pattern onto the tracing paper with a regular pencil. Also draw the outside circle.

2. Turn the tracing paper over and draw over the design using the tailor's chalk. (If you prefer, use a #2 pencil instead of tailor's chalk for all but the outer circle. It doesn't rub off as easily while you work.) Put a blank piece of paper underneath or you'll get faint pencil lines on your working surface. Then transfer the design to the fabric:

Trace the inner part first and work outward to avoid smudging the pattern with your hand as you work.

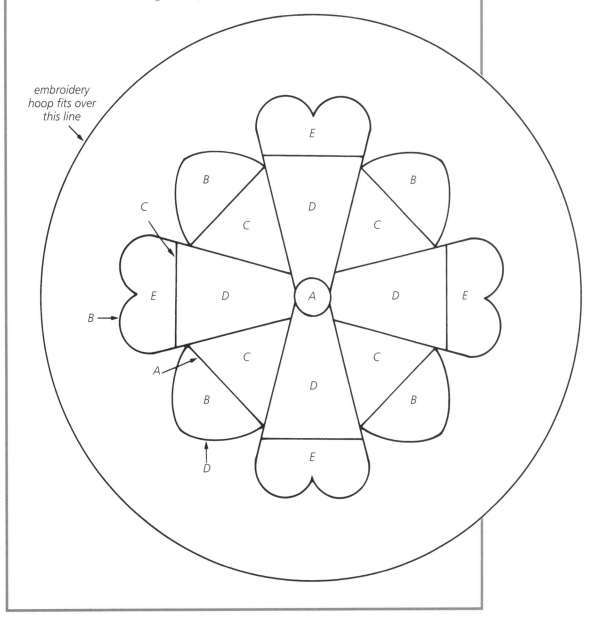

embroidery hoop fits over this line

Bead Embroidery

You could keep the knots at the back of the cloth, since you'll be hanging the embroidery or attaching it to a garment. In the interest of learning good beading habits, however, I recommend fastening the knot at the front, in a spot that will be covered by beads. The latter method is preferable for many embroidery projects, where exposed knots would rub against the skin, causing irritation to the wearer and putting strain on the knots.

3. Centre the tracing paper over the chamois or fabric, chalk side down. Draw over the design again with a regular pencil to transfer the chalk onto the chamois or fabric. Press lightly or the pencil will break the tracing paper.

Finally, attach the chamois or fabric to the embroidery or framing hoop (skip steps 4 through 7 if you're not using a hoop):

4. Separate the inner and outer rings of the hoop. Place the fabric over the inner ring, with the design centred and facing up. The circle of the pattern should line up with the ring.

5. Place the outer ring over the cloth and slide it into position around the inner ring. Keep the design centred.

6. Stretch the fabric tight by pulling on the protruding edges of cloth. On a regular embroidery hoop, tighten the screw on the outer hoop to hold the fabric firmly.

7. Trim away excess cloth, leaving about 1.3 cm (1/2 inch) all around for tightening the cloth as you work.

PREPARING THE THREAD
Repeat these steps whenever you run out of thread.

1. For beaded strands, use a doubled length of thread (needle in the middle) of a comfortable length. Use a single thread for couching (tacking) the beaded strands to the cloth. Make sure your thread is well waxed.

2. Knot the ends of the thread together, or if you prefer, make three small, overlapping stitches to secure the thread in a spot that will be covered by beads. Trim excess thread.

3. When you run out of thread or move to a new section of the fabric, secure the end with three small, overlapping stitches on a spot covered by beads. Trim excess thread.

EMBROIDERING THE DESIGN
You'll need two bead embroidery stitches for this design. They're described in the steps that follow (and in the "Bead Embroidery Stitches" section beginning on page 91).

Use the *back stitch* for forming the outlines of the four petals and four leaves, and fill the central circle and the outlines with the *couching stitch*. The pattern shows which colours to use for which sections.

Note: If you encounter problems as you work, see the working tips throughout this chapter for possible solutions.

Embroidering the circle at the centre of the flower

1. Secure a doubled thread to the cloth, half a bead's width from the centre of the circle in the middle of the flower.

2. Use the needle to pick up one A bead. Push the bead down the thread until it rests against the cloth in the centre of the circle.

3. Pass the needle through to the back of the cloth; it should go through directly in front of the A bead. Bring the needle up through the cloth a half-bead width away from the A bead.

4. Add enough A beads (about seven) to form a circle of beads around the central bead. Pass the needle through the first bead you added in this step and pull tight so the beads snugly encircle the central bead. (Note that the space between the beads is exaggerated in the diagram to show the movement of the thread.)

5. Secure a single thread to the cloth between the second and third beads you added in step 4. Make a small stitch over the thread between the two beads by passing the single thread over the doubled thread and then through to the back of the cloth. Don't pull the stitch so tight that it draws the doubled thread against the cloth; there should be a tiny gap between the doubled thread and the cloth, or the beadwork will have dents where you make the stitches. The couching stitch (also known as a tacking stitch) should be hidden between the beads.

6. Bring the single thread up between the fourth and fifth bead added in step 4. Make another small stitch over the doubled thread, and continue to couch between every second bead to anchor the circle securely to the cloth.

7. Make the final circle by stringing enough A beads onto the doubled thread to surround the beaded circle (about 15 beads). Don't forget to pass the needle through the first bead to hold the circle in place. Couch it to the cloth using the single thread. This bead-embroidered shape formed of concentric circles is called a *rosette*.

Don't worry if your bead embroidery doesn't look exactly like the pattern; sometimes the beads aren't fine enough, or the pattern isn't large enough, to create subtle curves.

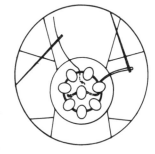

Bead Embroidery

8. Tie off the single thread by securing it to the cloth with three small stitches as described in "Preparing the Thread," then trim the excess.

Now you've finished the centre of the flower using the couching technique.

Embroidering the flower petals

1. Position the doubled thread at the front of the cloth beside the rosette, at the beginning of the outline of a petal (the four petals are scalloped at the outer edges).

2. Pick up three B beads and position them along the outline of the petal. Pass the needle through to the back of the cloth (in front of the third bead).

3. Bring the needle back up between the first and second bead and pass it through the last two beads again. (The space between the beads is exaggerated in the diagram to show the movement of the thread.)

4. Repeat steps 2 and 3 to cover the outline of the petal, ending when you reach the rosette again. You're using the *back stitch*. You can pass the needle through the third bead of each set, rather than the second and third, if you prefer. Tie off the threads.

5. Secure a new doubled thread at one end of the line that crosses the petal, dividing it into two sections (marked C on the pattern). Use C beads and the back stitch to embroider the line.

6. Add enough E beads to form a line of beads inside the petal's outline from one end of the cross-line around to the other end (see diagram).

7. Anchor a single thread to the cloth between the third and fourth E bead and use the single thread to couch the strand of beads on the doubled thread to the cloth. Make a couching stitch every third bead along the line.

8. Now add enough E beads to reach the beginning of the line of beads you added in the previous two steps; couch the beads to the cloth. Continue filling in the outer section of the petal by forming rows of beads inside the previous rows, working inward, with E beads and the couching stitch. This method of filling outlines by using consecutively shorter rows of beads is called contour beading.

9. Bring the doubled thread in position at the front of the cloth at one end of the cross-line on the unbeaded side of the petal (marked D on

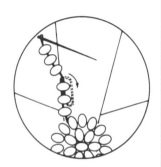

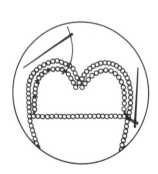

***You may find** you have some extra beads by the time you reach the cross-line because the couching stitches take up space. Whenever this happens, just remove the excess beads.*

the pattern). Add enough D beads to form a line of beads all the way around the inside edge of the unbeaded section of the petal and use the single thread to couch them to the cloth. (If it seems the distance from the previous section to the starting point for the new section is too far, tie off the threads and start this step with new threads.)

10. Continue contour beading, using D beads and the couching stitch, until the petal is filled in.

11. Repeat steps 1 through 10 to outline and fill in the remaining petals.

Embroidering the leaves

1. Outline the outer edge of a leaf with D beads and the back stitch.

2. Embroider the line that crosses the leaf and divides it into two sections with A beads and the back stitch.

3. Fill in the outer section of the leaf with B beads and the couching stitch (use contour beading).

4. Fill in the inner section of the leaf with C beads and the couching stitch (use contour beading).

5. Repeat steps 1 through 4 to embroider the remaining leaves.

FINISHING THE PROJECT

- If you used a framing hoop and plan to hang your beadwork, just trim away the 1.3 cm (1/2 inch) of cloth outside the hoop. Find a good spot to hang your picture and admire your work.
- If you used a regular embroidery hoop and want to hang your beadwork in it, trim away the outside 1.3 cm (1/2 inch) of cloth. Attach a loop of thread, wire or beads to the hoop's tightening screw. Hang your beadwork by the loop.
- If you want to sew your embroidery onto a jacket, T-shirt or other article, your next step depends on the cloth you used. If you used chamois or a nonfraying cloth, trim away the 1.3 cm (1/2 inch) of cloth outside the hoop. If you used a type of cloth that frays, don't trim this excess; you'll need it for hemming. Remove the beadwork from the hoop. Fold the excess cloth under, following the inner dent made by the embroidery hoop; if the cloth frays, fold it under twice to protect the raw edge. Sew the folded cloth in place. Then sew your finished beadwork to your article.

Sometimes when you couch the beads an oddly-shaped bead sneaks onto the thread. Or if you use a hoop, the beads may be too cramped once you take the hoop off. To remove malformed or excess beads, insert a large needle or an **awl** *into the bead hole to break the bead. Another method is to use pliers to break the excess beads. With either method, take care not to damage the thread. If using pliers, place the tips on either side of the top half of the unwanted bead* **above** *the thread; do not place one tip above and one tip below the bead, which would result in the crushed bead breaking the thread.*

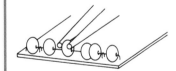

Materials

Some specialized materials—though you'll also use basic beading materials including beads, thread and needles—will make your bead embroidery easier. Here are some suggestions.

BEADS

Seed beads are the first choice for bead embroidery. Once you've practised the basic stitches with seed beads, however, try incorporating bugle beads, larger beads, sequins and buttons into your embroidery designs.

CLOTH

You can embroider beads onto almost any fabric. Chamois, lightweight leather, canvas, suede, felt, denim and velvet are particularly easy to work with; they don't stretch and are fairly sturdy. Avoid handling velvet too much, though, or the nap will wear and flatten. Also, choose a velvet with a short nap; beads will sink into a longer nap. Lighter materials such as silk and chiffon require a delicate touch, as they can easily pucker or tear. They may also reveal needle holes if you have to undo a mistake. On slightly stretchy materials like knit fabrics, embroider on areas unlikely to take strain, as such strain can distort your design or break the thread. Maintain even tension if you embroider on stretchy fabric; an embroidery hoop will help.

Dark-coloured materials will dull the look of the beadwork, particularly when you use transparent beads, because it absorbs the light.

Leather, chamois, canvas, felt and heavy cotton are good base materials for appliqué work.

Consider the fabric weight when you choose beads and a design. For example, heavy beads or a densely beaded design could cause a light fabric to tear.

EMBROIDERY HOOPS AND FRAMES

It's a matter of personal preference whether to use hoops and frames. Some beaders use them to keep their fabric taut and working area clear. Others feel they are more of a nuisance than a help, causing the beadwork to pucker once removed from the restraint, and making the fabric difficult to manipulate while beading, especially when beading only partway through leather. If you'd like to try hoops or frames to see for yourself, the following two paragraphs provide some guidelines.

Hoops are useful for small areas (such as rosettes) or lighter fabrics. Spread the fabric over

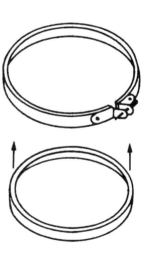

the inner ring, then place the outer ring in position over the fabric and inner ring.

For larger projects, construct a frame of the size you need. Nail four strips of wood together at the corners, or join them together using L-brackets. Tack the cloth tightly to the frame, if you can hide tack marks later. If you don't want to leave tack marks, use masking or basting tape (for fabrics without a nap) to fasten the material to the frame.

FRAMING HOOPS

These are embroidery hoops with an attractive finish and a loop at the top. Use circular and oval hoops for bead embroidery that you plan to hang, to avoid the necessity of transferring the finished beadwork to another frame.

MOCCASIN KITS

These handy kits contain everything you need to make your own bead-embroidered moccasins from scratch. Look for them at your beading or craft store. They come in different sizes, with instructions for applying beads and assembling leather pieces.

NEEDLES

The basic beading needle works well for most materials and is narrow enough to pass through thin leather quite easily. A special **glover needle**, with a very small eye and three-sided point, is useful for thicker leather. Another option for thick materials is to use an **awl** to punch holes for the needle to pass through.

TAILOR'S CHALK AND HEAT-TRANSFER PENCILS

These tools work well to transfer your design to the fabric. Choose a colour that contrasts with your material.

THREAD

Any fibre thread discussed in the *Tools and Materials* chapter will work for bead embroidery. As always, bear in mind the bead hole size. Also consider the fabric weight; use light thread for lightweight fabric and heavier thread for thicker materials.

TRACING PAPER

Use it to transfer your chalk or heat-transfer design to the fabric. You can also attach the tracing paper directly to the cloth and stitch through it.

Laundering bead-embroidered fabric. Hand wash or dry clean bead-embroidered fabrics to avoid wear and tear. The finish on some beads (such as metallic-coloured seed beads) comes off when exposed to water; test a few loose beads before hand washing. Also, check with your dry cleaner to ensure that the chemicals won't harm the beads. Never iron the beaded side of embroidered clothing. Iron the back of the garment, protecting it with a pillowcase or other cloth. Use the lowest heat setting to avoid melting plastic beads. Heat can also break glass beads.

If you're making a garment yourself and embroidering large areas, it's easier to do the bead embroidery before you sew the pieces of the garment together. Prewash the fabric so it doesn't shrink after you apply the beads.

Bead Embroidery

Preparing Your Design

Even the simplest pattern can become uneven or distorted when applied to the material without guidelines. If you plan to embroider a pattern already in the fabric or along a seam or edge, this may not be a problem. In most other cases you need to prepare your own guidelines and apply them to the cloth.

There are many different ways of transferring your design to the fabric. This section describes a few methods; use the one that appeals to you. The beads should cover the guidelines so they don't show once you finish. Some methods don't leave permanent marks, which allows you the flexibility to alter your design once you start beading. See Chapter 8, *Planning and Design*, for ideas about creating designs.

To create a symmetrical design, draw half of the design on the tracing paper. Then fold the tracing paper in half along the edge of the design, drawn side out, and trace the design onto the other half of the paper.

USING A HEAT-TRANSFER PENCIL
Draw the design on tracing paper using a heat-transfer pencil. Then simply position the pattern on the fabric drawn side down. Press with a heated iron to transfer the design to the fabric.

BASTING THE TRACING PAPER TO THE FABRIC
Draw the design onto the tracing paper with an ordinary pencil or pen. Baste the tracing paper to the fabric (using large stitches around the edges of the paper) and bead directly onto the tracing paper, passing the thread through both tracing paper and cloth. When you've beaded along the outlines, remove the basting stitches and tear away the tracing paper before filling in.

Another option is to baste or machine stitch the tracing paper to the fabric along the lines of the design, using a thread colour that contrasts with the fabric. Then rip away the tracing paper and use the basted or sewn stitches as your guidelines.

USING TAILOR'S CHALK
Draw the design on tracing paper with a regular pencil. Then turn the paper over and trace over the design with tailor's chalk. Position the tracing paper on the fabric, tailor's chalk side down, and trace over the design again using a pencil. This transfers the chalk to the material. You can easily rub these lines away; for more permanent guidelines, try using a #2 pencil in place of the tailor's chalk.

Bead Embroidery Stitches

The embroidery stitches described in this section are the ones traditionally used for bead embroidery. You can adapt other embroidery stitches for use with beads, however. When you plan your design, choose any stitch or combination of stitches that achieves your desired effect. And don't worry if your first results aren't perfect. Learning to embroider neatly can take a lot of practice! Here are some general guidelines to help you get started:

- When you embroider with beads, all knots should be on the outer side of the fabric. (See Chapter 10, *Basic Knots,* for information about tying knots.) This prevents the knots from wearing away as they rub against your skin. Position the knots where the beadwork will cover them or hide them inside the bead holes. The exception is beadwork attached to a backing which you appliqué to your garment. In this case, you can hide the knots between the backing and the garment.

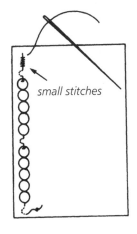

small stitches

- Another way of anchoring your thread is to make several small stitches on top of each other. This method is especially useful for securing the thread tail once you finish beading.

- Cut off the thread tail close to the knot or anchoring stitches before you begin to embroider.

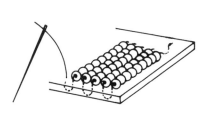

- If you are beading onto thick leather, sew just halfway through it and back out again, so no thread shows on the reverse side. This is especially important for shoes and gloves, where any thread on the inside would wear with use. Use the *lazy stitch*, described on page 94, if you are beading partway through leather, as other techniques eventually cause the design to distort.

- Use a doubled thread if you like (and always for the beaded strand when using the *couching stitch*), but bear in mind the number of times the thread must pass through the beads. Use as long a thread as you can comfortably work with. Wax your thread to prevent knotting.

- If your design has sections of beads in widely-separated areas, end the thread and begin a new one for each section. Avoid running threads for long distances under the cloth.

- After each stitch, make sure the thread at the back is not knotted or tangled. Not only is this messy, it may allow beads to loosen later.

Bead Embroidery

●When you remove the cloth from the tension of an embroidery hoop or frame, the beads will move closer together. To prevent your beadwork from bulging at this stage, bead solidly but without overcrowding. If the beads are too jammed when you take off the hoop, remove beads by breaking one or two. To avoid damaging the thread, see the working tip in the margin on page 87 for instructions.

BACK STITCH

You can use this stitch for straight or curved lines of beads. The project at the beginning of this chapter shows you how to use it to outline shapes. You can also use it as a filling stitch or to attach individual beads.

1. Secure the thread to the material. Begin with the needle and thread on top of the cloth, positioned at the beginning of the guideline.

2. Pick up one to three beads and push them down the thread close to the fabric, positioned along the guideline.

When you bead around a curve or corner, use fewer beads if necessary. You may need only one bead at time.

3. Push the needle down through the cloth slightly ahead of the last bead on the thread. Pull the thread tight, but not so tight that it puckers the cloth.

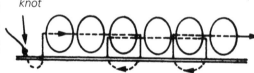

4. Push the needle up through the cloth behind the last bead and pass the needle through the last bead again.

5. Repeat steps 2 through 4 until you have covered the entire length of the guideline.

To use the back stitch as a filling stitch, embroider additional lines of beads inside the outer guideline, following the contour of the guideline and beading close to it, so no cloth shows. Add consecutively smaller lines of back stitch until the shape is filled in. This is called contour beading.

When you add a new thread, pass it through the last few beads before continuing to bead. This keeps the line of beads even, with no visible break.

COUCHING STITCH

This stitch is also known as the *overlay stitch.* Some beaders consider it a method of bead appliqué because it uses a separate thread to hold a strand of beads in place on fabric. The couching stitch produces the same results as the back stitch and *running stitch;* you can use it for outlines and as a filling stitch. (The bead embroidery sampler project at the beginning of this chapter shows you how to use it as a filling stitch.)

1. Use a doubled thread for the beaded strand. Anchor the thread to the cloth at the start of the guideline with the needle and thread on top of the cloth. Add enough beads to cover the entire guideline length.

2. Lay the beads along the guideline, but don't secure the end of the row. (You may need to remove some of the beads once you tack the line down.)

3. The tacking or couching thread should be a single thread. Fasten it to the cloth near the beginning and slightly to the side of the guideline. Bring the needle up between the second and third beads.

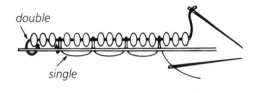

double

single

4. Making sure the strand of beads is positioned on the guideline, pass the couching thread over the beaded thread and through the cloth to make a small stitch. This holds down the strand, but don't pull too tight. The beaded thread should not touch the cloth, but rather pass freely between the two beads (otherwise the line of beads will have dips where each couching stitch is located). The couching (or tacking) stitch should be hidden between the beads.

5. Pass the second thread along the underside of the cloth and emerge three beads farther along the strand, or more frequently on a curved line. (You should tack the thread between every second bead if beading an outline.) Again, stitch the thread down between two beads.

6. Repeat step 5 until you've secured the strand all along the guideline.

7. Remove excess beads, if any. To anchor the end of the bead strand you can either make two tacking stitches after the last bead, or make a small stitch with the beaded thread, bringing the needle up where the next row will begin (if applicable).

LAZY STITCH

Apply the lazy stitch, also called the *lane stitch*, when you want to fill in outlines created with the *back*, *couching* or *running stitch*. You can also

Another use for the couching stitch is to create freeform designs: position a string of beads on the fabric, arranging it in different shapes until you find one that pleases you, then stitch it down.

You can also use the couching stitch to simultaneously add beads with one thread and make anchoring stitches with the second thread.

Bead Embroidery

use it without outlines to create solid shapes. Use the lazy stitch when you want to embroider on thick leather; this technique is ideal for beading partway through the leather.

1. Begin with the needle and thread on top of the fabric, secured at one corner of the shape.

2. Add enough beads to make a strand long enough to reach the other side of the shape. If this requires more than twelve beads, see the modified lazy stitch, next.

3. Pass the needle to the back of the cloth at the end of the strand (or partway through if beading on thick leather).

unbeaded sections of the pattern

4. Bring the needle up beside the last bead of the previous strand, where you want the next strand to begin. Reverse direction.

5. Repeat steps 2 through 4 until you've filled in the shape.

> *Use irregularly sized beads when necessary (there are usually some in every batch) to help create exactly the right line length.*

> *Use tight, even stitches. Space the lines so they're not bunched together, but don't leave gaps.*

Beading sections of lazy stitch

If the lazy stitch is more than twelve beads long it will hang or sag. To prevent this problem, you can bead as many sections of twelve-bead rows of lazy stitch as required to fill the shape. To make the sections form continuous rows, begin the first row of a new section twelve beads away from the end of the last row in the previous section. Add the beads for the new row, then pass the needle 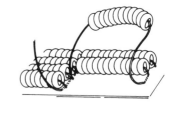 through the cloth, behind the anchoring stitches of the last and second-to-last row (see diagram). Bring the thread back to the front of the cloth, beside the anchoring stitch for the second-to-last row, and pull tight. This thread placement puts additional tension on the rows in the preceding section, helping to keep them flat.

Another option when the beadwork requires more than twelve beads is to use as many beads as needed to fill the shape, then modify the lazy stitch as described next.

MODIFIED LAZY STITCH

The modified lazy stitch is also called the *crow stitch*. Use it to prevent the beadwork from sagging if you've used rows of lazy stitch longer than twelve beads. To secure the lazy stitches in place, run threads across the beadwork at right angles to the lazy stitches. Space the cross-threads about five beads apart. Beginning at one end, pass the cross-thread under the first row of lazy stitch (under the cloth), emerging after the first row. Pass the thread back over the first row between two beads and through to the back of the cloth. This creates a couching stitch to anchor the lazy stitch in place. Continue adding couching stitches (without beads) until you have anchored each row of lazy stitch in place. Add as many cross threads as needed.

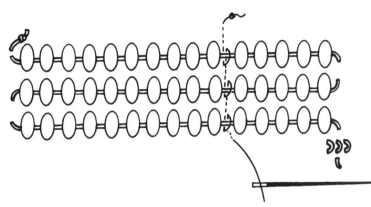

ROSETTES

Rosettes are bead-embroidered circles. There are two methods for forming rosettes, depending on the finished size.

For small rosettes, with a diameter of 2.5 cm (one inch) or less, work outward from the centre of the circle. (The project at the beginning of the chapter uses this rosette-making method to form the circle at the centre of the flower.) Begin by stitching a single bead or small circle of beads onto the cloth to form the centre. Add enough beads to snugly encircle the central bead(s) and pass the needle back through the first bead in the second circle. Use the *couching stitch* to fasten the second circle to the cloth. Continue adding larger circles and couching them to the cloth until your circle reaches the size you wish. The advantage with this method is that you are assured that the centre of the circle is filled solidly with beads.

Another method, recommended for larger rosettes, is to first couch a row of beads to form the outline of the circle. Couch the next row snugly against the inside of the outline, and continue to couch successively shorter rows inside the outline until you reach the centre. (Beading rows inside an outline to fill a shape is called contour beading.) This method is preferable for large rosettes because it ensures that the outer edge is a perfect circle (whereas beading from the centre out will magnify the slightest distortion, so by the time you reach the outer edges your circle is lopsided).

Bead Embroidery

RUNNING STITCH

The running stitch is the same as the *back stitch*, but it allows you to add four to eight beads at a time. A drawback is that it's harder to control the flatness of the beadwork. As with the back stitch, pass the thread backward under the cloth, then bring it to the front and go through half of the beads again. If you add six beads, for example, pass the thread through the last three beads before adding the next six.

SCATTER STITCH

The scatter stitch, also known as the *single stitch* or *tacking stitch*, adds one bead at a time. Use it with (or instead of) other filling stitches to fill in small or awkwardly shaped outlines, or use it alone to create a scattered bead effect. Try the scatter stitch with beads, sequins or buttons.

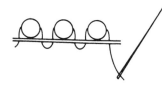

OTHER BEADED EDGINGS AND DESIGNS

Many other embroidery and beading techniques can be adapted to create beautiful edgings and designs. Use them to sew two edges of fabric or leather together, or add them afterward to cover exposed seams or decorate edges. Here are some ideas:

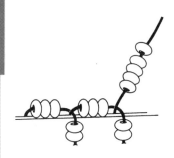

Blanket stitch is a traditional stitch used along a fabric edge. Begin with your needle close to the front edge. Add five beads and pass your needle from the back to the front of the fabric, directly in front of the third bead, but behind the thread that passes from the third to the fourth bead (see diagram). The fourth and fifth beads should be at the back of the material. Repeat until you've covered the desired distance. You can alter the proportion of beads you use to make the blanket stitch (for example, four in front, two in back).

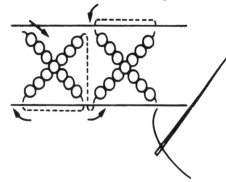

Cross stitch can be used for an edging or as a design anywhere on your fabric. Mark the back of your cloth with two parallel guidelines, or one guideline if you're embroidering along the edge. The cross stitch does not cover the guideline, so don't mark the front of your fabric. Begin with your needle on top of the cloth, positioned at the beginning of one of the guidelines. Add enough beads to create a diagonal stitch that reaches the other guideline. Pass the needle to the back of the material and bring it up at the beginning of the other guideline. Add the same number of beads as before and make a diagonal stitch that crosses over the first stitch (you may need to add an extra bead to achieve the same length). Pass the needle through the fabric, bringing it up level with the end of the first stitch.

Daisy stitch is a variation of the *couching stitch*. Embroider daisies along the hem of a garment, as part of an embroidered design or anywhere else you like. Begin by anchoring one bead or a small circle of beads to your cloth to form the daisy's centre. Bring the needle up beside the centre. Add enough beads to form a loop for the first petal. Pass the needle back through the fabric beside the beginning of the petal. Bring the needle back up at the outer edge of the loop; make a small stitch to secure the loop. Pass the needle behind the material to the start of the next petal. Continue adding petals until your daisy is complete.

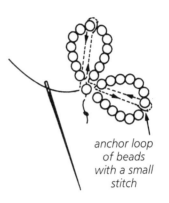

anchor loop of beads with a small stitch

Fringes can adorn the edges of scarves, shawls, pockets, yokes, the backs of jackets or any other area you like. Combine seed beads, bugle beads and larger beads. Alternate colours and vary dangle lengths to create different effects.

Attach fringes to the hem or along a seam. Secure each dangle with a small stitch in the fabric and run the thread along the back or inside the hem to the next spot where you want a dangle. Or use the *running stitch* or *back stitch* to add beads until you reach the next spot where you want a dangle. See the *Earrings* chapter for more ideas about using dangles to create fringes.

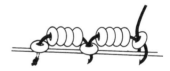

Loop edging, also called *scalloped edging*, makes a pretty trim. Begin with your needle close to the front edge of the cloth. Add six beads, then pass your needle through the fabric to the back. Bring the needle back up through the fabric and through the sixth bead. Add five beads and repeat, from now on adding five beads at time. Of course you can use different numbers of beads to achieve different effects. You can also pass the needle back up through two or more beads instead of just one.

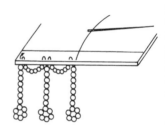

Overcast stitch, also called *whipped* or *rolled edging*, can join two edges of material or be used afterward as a trim. Begin with your needle about 0.6 cm (1/4 inch) from the front edge of the fabric. Add enough beads to reach around the edge of the material and cover 0.6 cm (1/4 inch) of the back side. Pass the needle through to the front of the cloth beside the first stitch. Repeat until you've covered the entire edge of the fabric with tight, even rows of beads.

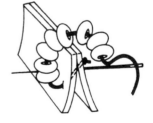

Bead Embroidery

Bead Embroidery

Peyote edging can trim your clothing; it's especially nice as a fancy addition to cuffs. Begin with your needle 0.15 cm to 0.3 cm (1/16 inch to 1/8 inch) from the front edge of the fabric. Pick up a bead and pass the needle through the cloth from front to back, bringing it back to the front the same distance from the edge and one bead-width farther along. Repeat, adding beads one at a time along the entire edge to form the base row. After you stitch the last bead in place pass the needle back through it. Add a bead and pass the needle through the second-to-last bead. Continue adding beads for the full length of the edging. When you've passed the needle through the first bead in the base row, if you want to bead a third row, add two beads then pass the needle through the last bead in the second row. Continue adding beads to complete the row. Add as many rows of beads as you wish, always using two beads at the beginning of a new row (each row should have the same number of beads). Notice that only the first row of beads is anchored directly to the cloth.

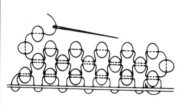

Stacked edging forms a solid edging. Begin by anchoring the thread near the edge of the fabric, with the needle emerging on the top side. Pick up four beads, and pass the needle through the cloth one bead-width away. Bring the needle back up through the last two beads, to form two "stacks" of two beads each. For the remainder of the edging, add two beads at a time, pass the needle through the cloth a bead-width away, then back up through the two beads again. You can vary the number of beads in the stack to achieve different effects.

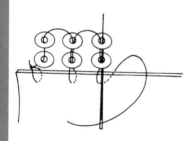

Zipper edging, attached along the outer edge of the cloth, creates a zigzag effect. To begin, anchor your thread at the edge of the material, pick up a bead and pass the needle through the cloth, one bead-width away from the anchor, and 0.3 cm (1/8 inch) from the edge. Bring the needle directly through the bead so it rests on the edge of the fabric, with the thread forming a loop that pierces the cloth below the bead. Add two beads, and again pass the needle through the cloth, the same distance away as before, then through the third (lower) bead. Pull tight, causing the second bead to stand up vertically, creating a zipper effect. Continue adding two beads at a time.

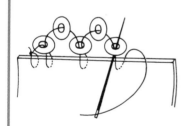

You can combine this technique with the *stacked edging* to create a *stacked zipper edging*, by following the stacked edging instructions but using five beads the first time (passing the thread back through the last two), and three beads for the remainder of the length.

Chapter Six
Other Things You Can Bead

This chapter describes additional things you can create with beads, using techniques you've already learned and some new findings. After you've tried a few earlier projects and feel ready to test your skills in new areas, try your hand at rings, barrettes and other hair accessories, brooches and pins, dream catchers and other types of wall hangings. They're fun to bead and can make perfect gifts.

Rings

Rings are always popular, and they're quick and easy to make. This section describes several ring-making methods, both with and without **ring findings** (metal rings to which you attach beads). Rings also double as scarf slides; just pull both ends of your scarf through the ring and slide it into position.

BEAD WOVEN RINGS

Off-loom and loom weaving are both great for making rings. A ring is a good way to try a new technique. It's so small it won't take long to see if you like the results, yet it gives you something to show for your efforts. Here are a few tips:

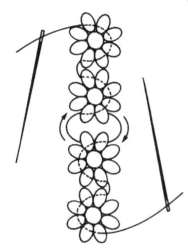

- Try using elastic thread for a flexible fit. Choose thread small enough to fit through the bead holes.
- It you use an off-loom weaving technique such as the *brick stitch, chevron stitch, daisy chain, ladder stitch, peyote stitch* or *square stitch,* (the diagram shows the daisy stitch), leave a thread tail of at least 15 cm (6 inches) at the beginning of the beadwork. When you've made the piece long enough to fit around the wearer's finger, weave the end thread onward through the beginning to make a continuous piece (see diagram). Then put the needle on the thread tail from the beginning of the beadwork and weave it through the end. This makes a neat, secure finish. For extra strength you can weave both tails through the entire ring, effectively tripling its strength. See Chapter 3, *Off-Loom Weaving,* for information about different off-loom stitches.
- If you're loom weaving the ring, first measure the wearer's finger. Make the beadwork one row longer than this measurement. Weave both tails of thread into the beadwork, then remove the work from the loom and apply the clean-edge finish for continuous pieces (described on page 76). You'll notice that loom weaving a ring wastes a lot of thread; your warp threads need to be much longer than the ring requires so you can attach them to the loom. Although people have used looms to make rings, a much easier way is to use the *square stitch* off-loom weaving technique; it achieves similar results without waste. Or construct your own tiny loom sized especially for making rings. See Chapter 4, *Loom Weaving,* for information about making a loom.

FLAT-PAD RING FINDING

This ring finding is an adjustable ring with a flat pad to which you attach beads or beadwork.

Here are a few ideas for using this finding:

- Glue a cabochon onto the pad to make a new ring in seconds flat. See "Using Jewellery Findings" in Chapter 2, *Earrings,* for tips on attaching cabochons to flat pads.

- Sew a circular piece of beadwork onto a fabric backing and sew the edges of the fabric around the back of the flat pad. See "Sewing onto Cloth or Leather" in Chapter 4, *Loom Weaving,* for more information. See Chapter 3, *Off-Loom Weaving,* for information about making circular shapes.

If you're sewing beadwork onto a pad, make sure you hide any knots between the cloth and the pad, or weave the thread back into the beadwork and knot it there. This prevents the knots from irritating your finger or coming undone with wear.

SCREENED DISK RING FINDING

Another type of ring finding has a curved metal disk with holes in it, or a fine wire oval of mesh. You may have to ask your bead store to special order this hard-to-get finding. Secure beads to the finding by sewing through the holes in the disk or mesh. See "Using Jewellery Findings" in Chapter 2, *Earrings,* for more information about using screened disk findings.

Barrettes and Other Hair Accessories

There are many ways to bead barrettes and other hair accessories. Most techniques described here use a basic barrette finding, which comes in various sizes. First, some general guidelines for working with the barrette finding:

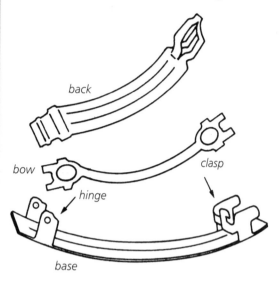

- The finding consists of a back, bow and base (see diagram) with holes in the base for securing beadwork. Disassemble the barrette into three pieces before attaching the beadwork.
- Once you've attached the beads or beadwork to the base, using one of the methods described in the following sections, reassemble the three pieces of the barrette.
- You can cover the metal base before attaching the beads, if you like, with cloth that matches your beads.
- Another option is to cover the base by wrapping it with a leather or suede lace before attaching the beadwork.
- When you wrap the base and attach beadwork, be sure to leave the clasp and hinge free so you can reassemble the barrette finding.
- The techniques described next work best with 26-gauge wire, though you can use strong nylon thread for small beads.

If you find that sections of the base are still exposed after you attach the beads, you may want to take the beads off and wrap the base with cloth or a lace before reattaching the beads.

ATTACHING A LENGTHWISE STRAND OF BEADS

This is an easy way to make a barrette. Cut a piece of wire two and a half times as long as the barrette base. Pass the tail of the wire through the hole at one end so that it extends halfway down the back of the base. String on enough beads to cover the base, then pass the wire through the hole at the other end. Knot or twist the two tails of wire together. You can apply **adhesive** to the twisted wire for an extra secure fastening. Reassemble the barrette finding.

ATTACHING WIDTH-WIDE ROWS OF BEADS

This method takes a bit longer than a simple lengthwise strand, but it affords an opportunity to create wonderful textured effects. It also covers more of the barrette finding.

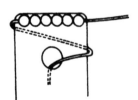

Insert a tail of wire through the hole at one end (with the tail at the back). Wrap the wire around the back of the base and position the remaining wire at the front end of the base. String enough beads on the wire to cover the width of the base. Wrap the remaining wire around the back of the base, then add beads at the front again. Continue wrapping the wire around the back and adding beads at the front to create a series of rows. You can leave gaps between the rows, if you like, and add a second series of rows to cover the gaps. Or weave rows diagonally in opposite directions. Use different sizes of beads and vary your row placement to create your own effects.

After you finish adding beads, pass the wire through the hole in the base and wrap it around the cross-wires several times to secure it. Then cut off excess wire. Reassemble the barrette finding.

If you like, string on all your beads first. Kink the wire so they won't fall off, then slide beads across the base front as you need them.

SEWING ON WOVEN BEADWORK

Off-loom and loom woven beadwork pieces make gorgeous barrettes, particularly when you make a bottom side fringe. Size the beadwork to completely cover the barrette base and use nylon thread to attach it, using one of the methods described next. See Chapter 3, *Off-Loom Weaving*, for information on different off-loom weaving stitches. See Chapter 4, *Loom Weaving*, for information about attaching side fringes to loom woven beadwork.

Materials that don't fray include chamois, leather, suede and felt.

Here are a few methods for attaching woven beadwork to the barrette base:

- Back the beadwork with fabric extending about 0.6 cm (1/4 inch) beyond its edges. (Allow extra fabric for a hem if you're using a fabric that frays.) Cut four notches in the fabric so it doesn't cover the hinge and clasp when you attach it to the base (see diagram). Hem the material, if necessary, then wrap the fabric around the base, with the beadwork facing out at the front of the base. Sew the fabric edges together at the back of the base, as shown in the diagram. See "Sewing onto Cloth or Leather" in Chapter 4, *Loom Weaving*, for information about sewing your beadwork onto a fabric backing.

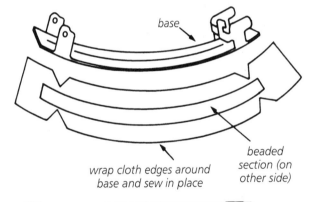

base

beaded section (on other side)

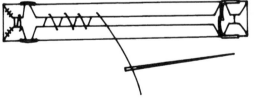

wrap cloth edges around base and sew in place

- Sew the beadwork onto a cloth backing, trim the cloth's edges even with the beadwork (if you're using a fabric that frays, hem edges under the beadwork), then glue the cloth directly to the base with an **adhesive** that bonds both fabric and metal, such as Bond 527 Multi-Purpose Cement®. Carefully put a heavy object on top of the beadwork while the adhesive dries, or temporarily sew the beadwork to the finding (as described next), to ensure the two parts bond securely.

- To attach the beadwork directly to the base, weave a thread into the beadwork, emerging next to a hole in the base (position the beadwork on the base to see where the hole will be). Pass the thread through the hole in the base, around the side and back through the beadwork. Repeat several times on both sides of the hole, then repeat for the hole at the other end. (See the diagram on the next page for sewing beadwork to a bar pin brooch.)

OTHER BEADED HAIR ACCESSORIES

You can also brighten hair combs, scrunchies and hairbands with beads.

- Glue woven beadwork, with or without fringes, to plain plastic hair combs.
- Cover a stiff hairband with the *peyote stitch* to transform it from boring to beautiful. (See Chapter 3, *Off-Loom Weaving*, for instructions on this stitch.)
- Sew beads along the outer edge of hair scrunchies. Leave the elasticized inner part plain so you don't stretch or break the beading thread.
- Embroider a beaded pattern on cloth hairbands. Embroider loosely; the hairband may stretch. See Chapter 5, *Bead Embroidery*, for information on preparing a pattern and using different embroidery stitches.

Brooches and Pins

Brooches and pins, though often overlooked as fashion accessories, add style and verve to any outfit. Wear them on your lapel or hat, or use them to hold a scarf in place.

BAR PIN BROOCH

This handy finding has a metal bar with several holes for holding beadwork, and a pin on the back. Bar pin brooches come in many sizes; longer bars have more holes.

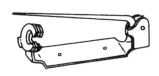

To attach off-loom or loom woven beadwork directly to the bar, weave a thread into the beadwork, emerging next to a hole in the bar (position the beadwork on the bar to see where the hole will be). Pass the thread through the hole in the bar, around the side and back through the beadwork. Repeat several times on both sides of the hole. Repeat for each hole. If you have backed your beadwork with fabric, attach it to the pin using one of the methods described for barrettes earlier in the chapter.

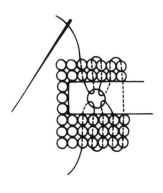

If your woven beadwork is larger than the bar pin brooch, you may want to stiffen the beadwork before attaching it, to prevent the edges from sagging. One way is to run short lengths of thin wire through the beadwork (inside the beads) to reinforce it.

For an interesting three-dimensional effect, thread clusters of beaded head pin dangles through the holes in the bar pin brooch, twisting the ends together at the back to secure them. (The dangle earrings project in Chapter 2, *Earrings*, gives information on making dangles.)

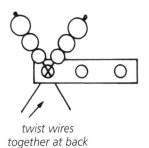

twist wires together at back

FLAT-BACKED BROOCH

A flat-backed brooch finding consists of an oval metal plate with a pin on the back. Attach woven beadwork or cabochons to flat-backed brooches as you would to flat-pad rings (see page 101), but make sure to leave the pin free.

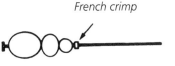

HAT PINS AND STICK PINS

The easiest pin imaginable is a few beads threaded onto a hat pin or stick pin. Use a **French crimp** or **adhesive** to hold the beads in position. If you use a French crimp, use pliers or a crimping tool to squeeze the crimp into place. You can use a shorter pin to make a tie-tack.

French crimp

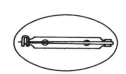

LONG BROOCH

In this method you use a hat pin, stick pin or length of 14-gauge wire. Bend the pin with needle-nose pliers to form a right angle about 0.6 cm (1/4 inch) from the head. Form the short end of the wire into a small loop that doesn't quite close. String beads on almost half the remaining wire. After the last bead, bend the wire again so it lies flat against the beads. Hook the end of the wire through the loop to secure the pin.

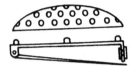

SCREENED DISK BROOCH

A screened disk brooch finding has a curved metal disk with holes in it, or an oval of fine mesh or wire, and a pin on the backing. Use head pins, 26-gauge wire or thread to attach beads to the disk. You can also attach beads to fancy filigree brooches; just use beads in selected spots so the beauty of the filigree shows through. See "Using Jewellery Findings" in Chapter 2, *Earrings*, for more on screened disk findings.

Wall Hangings

Many modern beaders apply their bead weaving and bead embroidery skills to wall hangings. Some hangings are extremely complex, but yours needn't be. Dream catchers, for instance, are popular, beautiful and easy to make.

DREAM CATCHERS

Some native North American peoples believe bad dreams get caught in the dream catcher's web, while good dreams flow through the centre. Bead one to hang by your bed or make dream catchers on specialized dream catcher ear hoops (called **pinched hoops**) to create a great pair of earrings. All you need is a metal hoop (or ear hoops), a few beads, and artificial sinew, embroidery silk, or leather, suede or cotton laces (or a similar cord that doesn't fray). Kreinik polyester metallic cord works well for earrings. This section describes one way to make dream catchers.

First cover your hoop with cord. Leaving a 15 cm (6 inch) tail, begin by temporarily knotting one end of the lace to the hoop with an *overhand knot*. (See Chapter 10, *Basic Knots*, for instructions on knots.) Wrap the thread all the way around the hoop. About halfway around, knot your web cord to the hoop, covering the knot with the wrapping cord. When you reach the beginning again, untie the overhand knot and tie the two tails of thread into a *square knot*, snugly against the hoop. Then knot the tails together with an overhand knot, about 5 cm (2 inches) above the first knot, to form a hanging loop. Trim excess cord.

Now fill in the hoop with a web of thread and beads. Using the web cord, make a *half-hitch* a short distance along the hoop; the shorter the distance, the tighter the web will be. Space the half-hitches at even intervals so the loops are the same size. Six to eight half-hitches usually work well for the first row if you're using a small hoop or ear hoops; use up to ten half-hitches for larger hoops. Continue forming loops and tying half-hitches until you return to the first one; leave the gap between it and the last loop about half as wide as for the other loops. Form the next row of loops by half-hitching the cord to the first row loops. Position the half-hitch in the centre of the previous row's loops. Add beads to any or all of the loops as you continue to work inward. Once you finish adding rows of loops to form the net and have reached the centre, tie the end of the web cord to a loop using an overhand knot (if you like, hide the knot inside a bead). Secure it with **adhesive** and trim away excess cord.

> **Use embroidery silk** *for dream catchers with small beads such as seed beads. If the silk is too thick to fit through the bead holes, separate the strands of the silk and use a single strand.*

> **Tie fringes** *of beads and feathers to the hoop bottom or fasten scattered feathers throughout the web to make your dream catchers even prettier.*

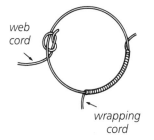

web cord

wrapping cord

> **For different effects,** *string on enough beads to completely cover each loop or pass the thread back through single beads after you form the half-hitch. You can also attach loops of beads around the outer edge of the hoop or edge the hoop with an off-loom weaving technique such as* **netting** *or the* **peyote stitch***.*

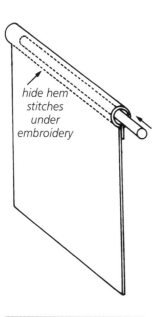

hide hem stitches under embroidery

On loom woven pieces, you can use an outer warp thread at the top end to make a cord. Allow enough length for this when you prepare the warp threads. Remove the beadwork from the loom and apply the clean-edge finish, leaving the longer outer warp thread free. Use the free warp thread to make a cord, as described to the right.

If you'd like to hang your beadwork in the window, use transparent seed beads and hang crystals from the fringe at the bottom to make a pretty sun catcher.

EMBROIDERED HANGINGS

You can make bead embroidered hangings with an oval or circular **framing hoop**, or hang the finished embroidery in the regular **embroidery hoop** you made it in. See Chapter 5, *Bead Embroidery,* for ideas. If you want to make a square or rectangular hanging, sew the top of the fabric over in an open-ended hem, hiding the stitches in the embroidery if possible. Slide a rod or wooden dowel into the hem, then attach a beaded cord as described in "Narrow Woven Bead Hangings," next. You can add a bottom fringe if you like. See "Other Beaded Edgings and Designs" in Chapter 5 for suggestions. A quick and attractive way to make fringes is to add two rows of overlapping loops of beads.

NARROW WOVEN BEAD HANGINGS

Narrow pieces of beadwork make beautiful wall hangings. All you need to do is attach a beaded cord at the top. Weave a thread through your beadwork to secure it, emerging from a top outer bead. Add seed beads until you reach half the desired length for the cord. The cord should be long enough that both ends meet the beadwork at an angle of at least 45° as shown in the diagram. A shorter cord will create too much tension on the beadwork, causing the edges to curl. Add a larger bead (make sure the seed beads don't fit inside the hole of the large bead), then enough seed beads to form a small loop. Then pass the needle through the larger bead again and pick up the same number of seed beads as for the first half of the cord. Pass the needle through the outer bead on the other side to anchor the cord. Then weave through several rows of beadwork, emerging from the top outer bead on the first side. Pass the thread again through all the beads of the cord, including the loop, to strengthen the cord. To finish, weave the thread through several rows of beadwork, knot the thread between two beads, run it through a few more beads and trim the excess thread.

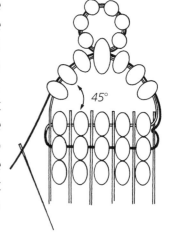

45°

WIDER WOVEN BEAD HANGINGS

On wider bead woven pieces, the beadwork will curl inward or sag unless you mount the top edge on a wooden dowel or rod. You can mount beadwork in many different ways. Most work equally well for large off-loom or loom woven pieces. Here are a few ideas. Also see the working tip in the margin on page 105.

Other Things You Can Bead

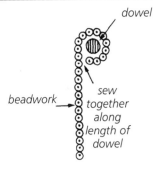

- Make the piece long enough to wrap the top part around the dowel. Sew it in place by weaving through the beads of the outer row and the main body.

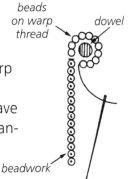

- For loom woven beadwork, leave the top warp threads loose and put enough beads on the threads to wrap around the dowel. Then weave the warp threads into the work using the clean-edge finish (described on page 76).

- Use a new thread to mount the beadwork onto the dowel (first apply the clean-edge finish to the top warp threads if the beadwork is loom woven). Weave the new thread through the beadwork, emerging from the outer bead in the top row. Add enough beads to cover the dowel and weave down into the beadwork, then back up through the second bead. Repeat to add a loop of beads for each bead in the top row and an extra loop at the farther edge (or just space loops periodically across the top). Vary the distance that you weave into the beadwork each time to distribute the stress through several rows.

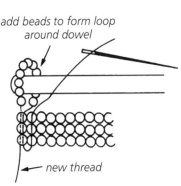

- If you want to make a hanging using *anchored netting* or the *right-angle weave*, anchor the threads to the dowel before you begin beading.

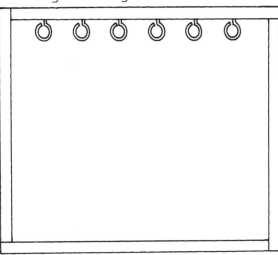

- Screw eye hooks to hang down from the top piece of a wooden frame; suspend beadwork from the hooks.

Chapter Seven

Making Your Own Beads

If you've ever searched fruitlessly from store to store, looking for a particular shape or colour of bead but unable to find it, you'll be happy to know that you can easily make your own beads. Someone has to make them, and who knows what you want better than you?

Making your own beads is inexpensive and fun. Best of all, you'll know your beads are truly unique. This chapter covers two simple bead-making techniques using paper and polymer clay.

Paper Beads

Paper beads are simple to make and require just a few materials that you probably have around the house. As an added bonus, making beads from paper lightens your load for the recycling depot!

MATERIALS

Core. You need something to form the bead around so the finished bead will have a hole in the middle for stringing. Choose an object that will create the size of hole you need. Round wooden toothpicks work well for small holes (don't use tapered, flat toothpicks; they make it difficult to roll the paper evenly). For a bigger hole use a knitting needle, wooden dowel, nail or similar object.

Finish. You don't need to paint the finished beads, but you can paint them if you prefer a uniform colour. You may choose to protect paper beads from moisture by applying a colourless finish like clear nail polish, shellac or other varnish.

Glue. Any kind of **adhesive** that works with paper will do. A glue stick like Elmer's® is especially handy. If you choose liquid glue or wallpaper paste you'll need something to spread it with, perhaps a paint brush or rubber spatula.

Paper. You can use any kind of paper; different kinds produce different effects. Suggestions include glossy paper from colour magazines, corrugated cardboard, leftover scraps of wallpaper, coloured construction paper and newspaper that's a few days old and slightly yellow (for an antique effect).

Pencil. For marking lines on the paper.

Scissors or hobby knife. For cutting paper strips to make the beads. A hobby knife such as an exacto knife can let you work more quickly and form straighter lines—after some practice—but scissors work too. Another option is to use pinking shears (dressmakers' scissors with serrated edges) to create a zigzag effect.

Straight-edge. If you plan to use a hobby knife to cut your strips of paper, use a metal ruler. Otherwise you can use a plastic or wooden ruler, or any other straight-edged tool.

Making Your Own Beads

PREPARING THE PAPER

Preparing the paper involves cutting it into strips to yield the shape of bead you want. The easiest shapes to achieve are oval, cone-shaped and cylindrical beads.

Oval. To make an oval bead, cut your paper into long isosceles triangles. The length of the base of the triangle determines the length of the finished beads, so mark out your strips accordingly. There's an easy way to make sure your strips are all the same size (and to use the full sheet of paper). Mark the right-hand side into segments of the length you want the bead to be, for example 1.3 cm (1/2 inch). Make your first mark on the left-hand edge of the paper half this length, for example 0.65 cm (1/4 inch). Then make the remaining marks on the left side the same distance apart as the marks on the right side, for example 1.3 cm (1/2 inch). Draw lines to connect the marks (see diagram). Cut out the strips and discard the top and bottom strips; the remaining strips will all be exactly the same size and shape.

If you use a straight-edge and hobby knife to cut your strips, you don't need to draw the lines. Just mark the segments at the edges of the paper, connect them with the straight-edge and cut.

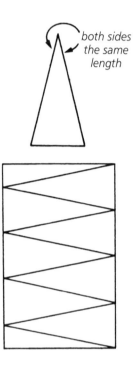

both sides the same length

Cone. To make cone-shaped beads, cut strips into long right-angle triangles. Again, the length of the base of the triangle determines the length of the bead. If you want a bead that's 1.3 cm (1/2 inch) long, mark out 1.3 cm (1/2 inch) segments along both sides of the paper (see diagram). Connect the marks to form rectangles, then draw a diagonal line through each rectangle to form right-angle triangles.

The length of the strip and the thickness of the paper determine the diameter of your bead; experiment until you find the right balance.

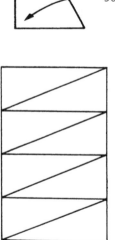

90°

Cylindrical. To form cylinder-shaped beads, cut strips into long rectangles. The width of the rectangle determines the width of the beads. Mark the paper as described for cones, but don't divide the rectangles into right-angle triangles.

FORMING THE BEADS

Once you've prepared the strips of paper, you're ready to make the beads.

1. Place your core at the wide end of the triangle, or one end of the rectangle, and wrap the paper around the core as shown in the diagram.

Cover your working area with newspapers to protect it from glue.

2. Cover the inside of the remaining paper with a thin layer of glue.

3. Tightly roll the paper around the core until you reach the end. On oval beads the paper should taper evenly on both sides. On cone-shaped beads the straight edge of paper should line up but the other side will taper. If you use rectangular strips, both sides should line up.

4. Remove the core.

5. Apply a protective finishing coat if you wish.

Now all that's left is to use the beads in your newest creation.

Making Your Own Beads

Polymer Clay Beads

You can make professional-looking beads of any shape, colour and design you want by oven-baking polymer clay. Several brands are available. Fimo® is the one you're most likely to find at your bead or craft store. Others include Sculpey® and Cernit®. Different brands have different pliability (Fimo is quite stiff, for example, while Sculpey is softer), but all polymer "clays" are actually made of plastic, which is why you can bake them at low heat in a regular oven. The clays come in many colours including metallic and transparent. Feel free to blend different brands and colours to achieve your own one-of-a-kind effects.

Polymer clay contains a plasticizer that makes the clay malleable. Residual plasticizer may leach out of the clay, leaving a potentially hazardous oily ring where the clay was sitting. For this reason, do not work the clay near food or food preparation surfaces, and be sure to wash your working surface, tools and hands carefully after working with the clay. Also wash your hands as you work, between colours, to prevent unplanned mixing of pigments.

Wrap your opened clay in waxed paper and store it in tightly closed plastic bags in a cool, dark area, as heat and light can partially bake the clay.

MATERIALS

Apart from the clay, most materials for making polymer clay beads are common household items.

Baking sheet. Bake the beads on this. Use one with a flat, smooth, non-heat-conductive surface such as a ceramic plate or Pyrex® dish.

Cutting tool. Cut the clay with a hobby knife such as an exacto knife, a razor blade or any knife with a thin blade. Another option is to use a thin wire to slice the clay. (You might want to attach a large wooden bead to either end of the wire to hold onto as you slice.)

Piercing tool. For making holes in the beads once you've formed them. Any pointed tool will do; sewing needles and round toothpicks are handy for small holes. Other possibilities include an awl or a knitting needle.

Rolling tool. This optional tool is handy for flattening the clay into smooth sheets, and for pressing two sheets together. Use a small rolling pin or even a glass bottle with the label removed. Note that the clay may stick to a wooden rolling pin, and pick up impressions from the wood grain; a marble or stone rolling pin works better. Another option is a printer's brayer. This handy roller with a handle attached to the ends is available in most art supply stores.

Other tools. Other optional tools for shaping the beads include cookie cutters and etching tools; use anything you can think of to press shapes or textures into the beads, creating your own special bead designs.

SOFTENING THE CLAY

Use the heat and pressure of your hands to soften stiff clay like Fimo®; this makes it shapable and easy to work with. Cut a small lump of clay from the block, and roll and knead it briskly between your hands. As the clay lengthens into a log shape, fold it in half and keep rolling and kneading until it is soft. Blend colours at this stage if you like. Colours mix as they would for paint; for example, red and blue blend to make purple.

SHAPING THE BEADS

You can shape beads by many different techniques. Use your imagination and flair for colour to create any number of designer beads. The steps that follow outline the basic steps and a few alternatives, but I'm sure you'll dream up many other ideas.

To achieve a marbled effect, partially blend two colours of clay. Take a lump of each colour; knead and fold the two colours together until you're pleased with the pattern (cut the lump open periodically to check).

1. Begin by forming a complex log (also known as a cane, or as a loaf if square or rectangular) by combining logs of different colours of clay. The shapes and colours you use to form the log will determine the beads' pattern. Here are some ideas:

- If you want beads of a single colour or marbleized clay you've already prepared, just shape the clay into a smooth log of even width and go to step 2.

- Layer sheets of alternating colour to achieve a striped pattern. Using your rolling tool, start at one edge and roll evenly to the opposite edge, to avoid air bubbles. (Air bubbles expand as the clay heats, leaving a hole which can weaken the bead.)

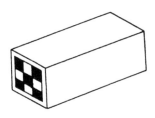

- Stack square logs, five of one colour and four of another, to form a checkerboard pattern. Ensure the logs adhere to each other along the entire length, to avoid gaps or air bubbles. Wrap the stacked logs with a sheet of clay to form a border around the checkerboard.

● To form a flower pattern, surround a round log with smaller logs in alternating colours. You can use triangular logs to fill the spaces in the outer circle of logs or wrap the whole thing with another sheet of clay.

● Cut a triangular log into five pieces and place these around a log of the same colour to form a star shape. Fill in the spaces between the points of the star with another colour.

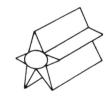

2. Cut your finished log or loaf into slices. Press the blade downward while shifting its pressure slightly from side to side against the clay to cut smooth edges.

3. Roll the slices into balls, cylinders, cubes, rectangles or any other shape you like. Roll the clay between your palms to form balls and cylinders or roll the slice on a smooth surface with your rolling tool to form cubes and rectangles. Notice that the pattern in the slice changes as you form the bead.

4. Pierce holes with a tool that will create the hole size you need for stringing the beads. Make the hole by twirling the tool as you press it through the bead, first halfway through on one side, then working from the other side, until the two holes meet. This method produces clean edges around the bead holes.

BAKING THE BEADS
This is the easiest part!

1. Place the baking sheet in the oven and preheat to the temperature called for on the clay package instructions. Lighter colours are more susceptible to burning. Use the temperature recommended for the lightest clay if the beads are predominantly a light or transparent colour.

Polymer clays are very sensitive to temperature. If your beads often burn or haven't hardened when baked for the recommended time at the recommended temperature, your oven's thermometer may be inaccurate. To solve the problem, purchase a good oven thermometer and check your oven's temperature throughout several heating cycles, then adjust the temperature setting accordingly.

2. Take the baking sheet out of the oven and place the beads on it in an upright position (with the hole running from top to bottom). The finished beads may have a shiny spot where they rest against the pan

---

Making Your Own Beads

Chilling the clay *makes it easier to slice.*

After you shape *the bead, you can add still more patterns by pressing thin slices of smaller logs onto the shape to form dots and circles. Roll the bead to make the new slices blend smoothly into the surface or leave them as they are for a raised effect.*

while baking. To avoid this problem, you can string the beads onto a wire and suspend it over the baking pan (as shown in the diagram). Another option is to line the baking pan with a clean sheet of white paper.

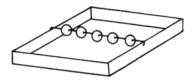

3. Bake for the length of time instructed for the clay. If you're mixing two brands of clay, add the two times and halve them to calculate an average baking time.

4. Remove the beads from the oven and allow them to cool.

5. Test the beads after they cool. If they're done they will be completely hard and make a sharp sound when rapped on your working surface. If they haven't hardened completely, they will feel like a firm grapefruit, yielding slightly when squeezed. If they're not done, return them to the oven for a bit longer at the same temperature.

Now admire your beautiful new beads!

***As the clay heats** in the oven, noxious fumes may be released (particularly if the temperature is too high). Be sure the area near your oven is well-ventilated. If a batch of beads burns, turn off the oven and carry the beads outside; avoid breathing any fumes. If you plan to do a lot of work with polymer clay, you may want to purchase a toaster oven to use exclusively for making beads.*

Making Your Own Beads

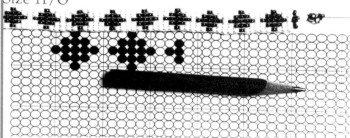

Loom Graph Paper
Size 11/O

Chapter Eight

Planning and Design

Designing beadwork can be as simple as mixing and matching beads, or as complex as mapping out a loom woven tapestry that will use thousands of seed beads.

It's exciting to walk into a bead store and look around for inspiration, or to sit down and work out a design on paper. Anything is possible! You can make anything you want, and you are the only one you have to please.

You already have some experience with planning and design if you've done any beadwork projects in this book. You planned which beads and colours to use, and perhaps how to arrange them.

Now you're ready to plan your own designs from scratch. This chapter takes you step by step through the complete planning process, including adapting your plan as you work. It also provides suggestions to help you come up with an idea if you're not sure how to begin. Before you know it, you'll be looking at your new beadwork creation.

Steps for Planning and Creating Your Design

COMING UP WITH AN IDEA

The first step to planning your project is to come up with an idea. You can focus on any aspect of beading: what you want to make, the beads you plan to use, a technique you want to try, or a colour or design you like. Honour your creative process; there's no single *right* way to begin. Decide on one element first. Don't worry about the rest yet; you just need the first spark. Here are some questions and ideas to get you started:

- Do you want to make something functional, like jewellery or other beaded accessories, or something purely decorative, like a wall hanging or dream catcher?
- Do you need something new to complement your wardrobe? What colours do you wear most often? Do you accessorize with brooches, barrettes or hairbands?
- Do you want to make a gift for a friend or family member? What colours or fashion styles does your friend like? What image or colour expresses your feelings about your friend?
- Would you like to try a new technique? Are you ready to extend your beading expertise? Pick a technique you've never done from the beading chapters in this book or the planning checklist (page 125).
- Do you have one marvellous bead that you'd like to use? Find other bead shapes and colours to complement it. Try combining beads of different materials, sizes and textures.
- Do you have old, little-used jewellery with tarnished metal beads, chipped glass beads, ugly repair knots or an old-fashioned style? Take it apart. Discard unsuitable beads, clean dirty beads, maybe add new beads and put it all together in a new and appealing form.
- Borrow ideas; glance through the photos in this book or other beadwork books. Choose a design that appeals to you: dragons, mythical castles, Egyptian kings and queens. Also, check out cross-stitch and embroidery books; the patterns adapt easily to woven beadwork and bead embroidery.
- Bead colours can evoke a particular culture. Silver and turquoise suggest the southwestern United States; gold and jewel tones evoke India. Your library is full of ideas.
- Do you dream or daydream in colours? Creation usually begins in the subconscious, so if an image or colour keeps coming to you, pay attention.

Planning and Design

●You may enjoy working with a colour you've never used before or finding new colour combinations. Unlikely colours can look wonderful together.

PLANNING THE DETAILS

Now it's time to fill in the details. You may have already chosen some or all of the design elements listed below; some may not apply to your project. (For example, if you're making earrings you probably don't need to worry about measurements.) Go through the list (in any order you like) to make sure you've planned everything necessary. Fill in the planning checklist (page 125) as you go to keep track of your selections.

Decide what you're going to make

Your chosen beads, technique, colour or design will narrow your options. Large or heavy beads may not be practical for earrings but could suit a necklace or bracelet. Bead weaving with the brick stitch could produce fringed earrings or a wider piece of beadwork like a wristband. A yellow and orange colour theme might suggest a sun shape suitable for a brooch or bead woven pendant. A complicated design would suit a larger piece of beadwork like a loom woven wall hanging or bead-embroidered T-shirt.

Pick colours and kinds of beads and thread

Your chosen beads and technique affect each other. Bead embroidery and bead weaving techniques are usually done with seed beads, for example, but you could also incorporate bugle beads or larger beads.

Thread can also be a design element. Normally you'd choose thread the same colour as the main beads so it doesn't show, but you can experiment with thread in a contrasting colour. Choose a cord that complements the beads if it will be exposed. Choose a thread suitable for your beads and technique. Off-loom weaving techniques generally need a thin fibre thread; heavy beads call for thicker cord or wire. See "Materials" in Chapter 1, *Stringing,* for more on threads.

Choose beading and finishing techniques

Choose a suitable technique. Large beads might suggest a stringing technique; smaller beads could suit an earring dangle, brooch or ring.

Combine techniques to achieve your desired shape, size and pattern. To make a beaded purse, you could form the body with *netting* or *peyote stitch* and the strap with stringing or loom weaving.

Also plan your finishing technique to include the right findings and enough thread. The "Finishing Techniques" sections in Chapters 1, 3 and 4 offer more information.

Write down measurements for the project

Measurements may be unnecessary for projects such as earrings or brooches, but in many cases they're a help. Knowing the length of a strung necklace will guide you in spacing the beads. Plan the width, too, for a wider piece of beadwork like a loom woven wristband or belt. If you're applying bead embroidery to a jacket, plan the area you want to cover and adjust your pattern accordingly.

How much room will your finishing technique take up? If you're using a crimp and clasp finish, line up the findings and subtract their measurement from your desired finished length to calculate the length of the beaded portion. If you want to apply end fringes to a piece of loom work, add to your warp threads double the length of the longest fringe (quadruple the length if you plan to make fringes at both ends) plus 15 cm (6 inches) at each end for weaving the thread in.

Finalize your design

Planning a design can involve arranging your beads in order, choosing a pattern, making a sketch or filling in the rectangles or ovals (one for each bead) on beading graph paper.

To plan a project like a necklace or brooch, you may only need to lay out the beads in different combinations on a bead stringing board or try stringing them on a thread.

For bead embroidery, you can borrow a pattern or draw your own. If you borrow, adapt the pattern to suit your project's size and shape. Trace the pattern using transfer paper and make any necessary adjustments. Then retrace. See Chapter 5, *Bead Embroidery*, for more on preparing your pattern.

A quick sketch to follow can help you bead a simple project. Draw some beads in the daisy chain pattern, for example, then try filling in different colours and patterns. If you have a beaded earring shape in mind, sketch it, then choose the size and shapes of beads.

Using Beading Graph Paper. For more complicated seed bead projects use beading graph paper to plan your design. Beading graph paper has been developed for loom work, brick stitch, netting, peyote stitch (both one- and two-drop) and right-angle weave. Peyote stitch graph paper can be turned 90° and used for the brick stitch, and vice versa; loom work graph paper can also be turned 90° and used for the square stitch. (The beads for the brick stitch and loom weaving are horizontal, while the beads for the peyote and square stitches are vertical.) Some types of beading graph paper use rectangles to represent the beads, and

If you're designing loom work, a general guideline for size 10° seed beads is to plan for 15 to 16 beads per inch in width and 11 to 12 beads per inch in length. If you have a rough idea of the size you want, you can sketch an outline of the piece on **beading graph paper**, then fill in a design.

If you're using laces, use a different thread while you decide on a stringing order. Adding and removing beads can ruin a lace's finish.

Keep adjusting the colours and patterns until you're satisfied. It's easier now than when you're beading, though you can adjust then too.

Planning and Design

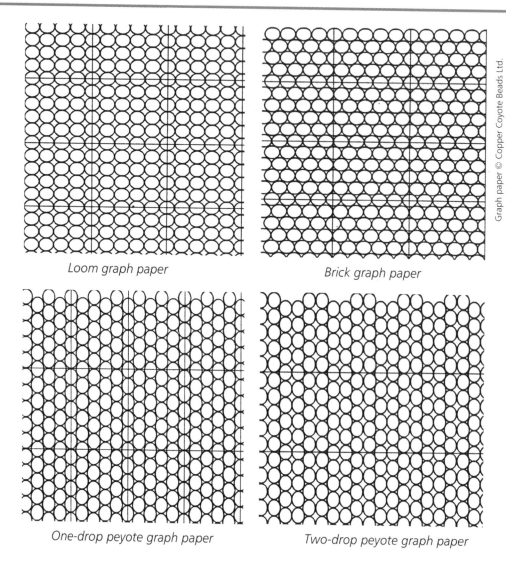

Graph paper © Copper Coyote Beads Ltd.

Loom graph paper

Brick graph paper

One-drop peyote graph paper

Two-drop peyote graph paper

***You might want** to prepare two copies of the pattern: one to the scale of the beads you're using, so you can make sure the design will result in the proportions you intend, and an enlarged version that is easier to work from.*

others use ovals. Some suppliers sell pads of beading graph paper, while others provide a reusable transparent template.

You can draw your design directly on the graph paper, or make a rough sketch first and transfer it to the graph paper. Fill in a rectangle or oval for each bead. Work out the shape first, then fill in different bead colours to finish your design. You may want to use pencilled symbols like Xs and Os to represent different colours so you can erase if necessary. Once you have the design you want, add colour.

Transparent templates are not meant to be drawn on; they're for use with a photocopier. They allow you to transform any image into a graphed design. Simply place the template over a photograph or sketch, then photocopy it. Depending on the quality of the photocopier, the original image, and the size of beads on the template, the photocopy may be ready to bead as is, or it may need further adjusting. Another alternative is to photocopy the blank template (reducing or enlarging it if necessary), then transfer your design to the graph paper.

Designing Fringes. If you want fringes, you can plan their pattern now or wait to see how the beaded portion turns out. You can use beading graph paper to design the fringes too; this is especially useful if you plan to incorporate a complicated design into the fringes. Have a rough idea of the length of the fringes so you can prepare enough thread (or you can add them later using a new thread).

Plan the materials and tools you'll need

Once you've chosen beading and finishing techniques, you'll know which findings, special materials and tools you'll need. Assemble everything before you begin so you won't need to stop beading to find them.

ADJUSTING YOUR PLAN

It's always exciting to see your design become reality, but it doesn't always turn out as you expect. Sometimes your beadwork looks even better than you imagined. But if you're not happy, take a deep breath and consider what's not working. It's a natural part of the creative process to rework your plan as you go. A few tips can help you adjust your design:

- Compare your beadwork to the pattern. Did you use the right colours without skipping a bead? If the beadwork differs from the pattern, undo it. Rework following the pattern exactly. It's easy to miss a bead, especially in a complicated pattern or technique.
- If you followed the pattern exactly and it still doesn't look right, don't despair. The design may not translate into beads the way you imagined; this is a hazard of working from a two-dimensional plan to three-dimensional beads. All kinds of things can go wrong: sometimes colours that look good together on paper don't look right when translated into beads; if your graph paper has a different height-to-width ratio than your beads, the proportion of colour or the shape of the design may be altered as you bead; irregularly sized beads may throw the pattern off; or different sections of beadwork may not fit together as planned.

    For every problem there's a solution. You can rework the pattern, change bead colours, reorder the beads, add spacer or filler beads, or discard some beads and add new ones. Experiment until the beadwork pleases you; accept only a satisfying design.

- Mechanical problems like running out of thread or breaking a bead are easy to correct; Chapter 9, *Solutions to Common Beading Problems* offers guidance.

*If you discover your finished beadwork isn't long enough with the clasp, extend it with **jump rings** or a new beaded section.*

Planning and Design

Are you having fun? If not, maybe it's time to take a break and come back to the beadwork refreshed. If you're feeling frustrated and encountering seemingly endless problems, it's a sure signal to stop. When you return to the beadwork, you may find the answers waiting for you!

Once you finish the beaded section, you may decide against your planned finishing technique. Perhaps you intended to use a **barrel clasp** which looks too clunky for a delicate piece; switch to a smaller clasp such as a **spring ring**. Or maybe you planned a clean-edge finish, but now you think a fringe would look better. If you don't have enough thread, add fringes with a new thread.

Making a plan doesn't mean you must follow it rigidly. Flexibility is a skill you'll develop as you create your beadwork designs. If your plan isn't working, you'll know soon enough and figure out how to change it. There's always a solution. You have all the skills you need and you'll learn more as you work. Trust your instincts. Be daring. Remember, if it doesn't work you can always start over!

PLANNING CHECKLIST

Shopping List

_____

_____

_____

_____

_____

_____

_____

_____

_____

_____

I'm going to make _____

(necklace, bracelet, earrings, ring, brooch, barrette, belt, embroidered T-shirt, etc.)

Colour(s) _____

Description of beads _____

Type of thread ❑ nylon ❑ silk ❑ tiger-tail ❑ monofilament/invisible ❑ lace ❑ wire ❑ other

Description of thread _____

Other materials ❑ clasp ❑ crimp ❑ jump/split ring ❑ earring findings ❑ eye pins ❑ head pins
❑ barrette finding ❑ brooch finding ❑ ring finding ❑ triangle ❑ fabric ❑ other

Description of materials _____

Tools ❑ scissors ❑ pliers ❑ tape measure ❑ wire snips ❑ file ❑ awl ❑ beading loom
❑ embroidery/framing hoop ❑ heat transfer pencil ❑ tailor's chalk ❑ other

Description of tools _____

Other supplies ❑ needles ❑ beeswax ❑ adhesive ❑ graph/tracing paper ❑ other _____

Beading technique(s)

Stringing	**Off-Loom Weaving**	**Embroidery**	**Embroidery Edges**	**Other**
❑ 3-strand braid	❑ 5-triangle circle	❑ back stitch	❑ blanket stitch	❑ cone & tassel earrings
❑ 4-strand braid	❑ brick stitch	❑ couching stitch	❑ cross stitch	❑ fringed earrings
❑ knotting/bead caps	❑ chevron stitch	❑ free-form	❑ daisy stitch	❑ glue to flat pad/bell cap
❑ multistrand	❑ daisy chain	❑ lazy stitch	❑ fringes	❑ head/eye pin dangle
❑ single strand	❑ ladder stitch	❑ modified lazy stitch	❑ loop edging	❑ sew to screened disk/bar
❑ twist	❑ looping stitch	❑ rosette	❑ overcast stitch	❑ triangle dangle
Loom Weaving	❑ mandala	❑ running stitch	❑ peyote edging	❑ wire spirals
❑ beaded warp	❑ netting	❑ scatter stitch	❑ stacked edging	
❑ regular	❑ peyote stitch		❑ zipper edging	❑ _____
❑ split	❑ right-angle weave			
❑ tapered	❑ square stitch			❑ _____

Description of technique _____

Finishing technique(s)

Bracelet/Necklace	**Loom Woven & Wider Beadwork**	**Other**
❑ bead fastener	❑ clean-edge finish	❑ beaded chain (for hangings)
❑ cone & head pin (to join multiple strands)	❑ cloth fasteners	❑ earring findings
❑ crimp & clasp	❑ end/side fringes	❑ sew onto cloth or leather
❑ end spacer (to join multiple strands)	❑ tapered beaded finish	❑ wire scrolls & S-links
❑ hook & chain		
❑ knot (square/sliding)	❑ other _____	❑ _____

Description of technique _____

Measurements: Length:_____ Width:_____ Other:_____

Notes: _____

_____

_____

_____

Sketch:

Planning and Design

Chapter Nine

Solutions to Common Beading Problems

Certain problems routinely occur when you're beading. This chapter offer solutions and tips for prevention; consult it if you have any problems when you try the techniques in this book. (If your problem is design-related, see "Adjusting Your Plan," in Chapter 8, *Planning and Design,* for suggestions.) As always, remember that the ideas here are just a few of the possible solutions. You may discover your own solutions and find that they work even better for you.

PROBLEM: Can't Thread the Needle

Cut the thread at an angle, trim away uneven fibres, wet the end of the thread and press it flat as you insert it in the eye. Your package of needles may include a threader, but use it with care; a threader can break the delicate metal surrounding the needle's eye.

PROBLEM: Beads Rolling Around

Create a portable work area by lining a cookie sheet with cloth. It's big enough to hold all your materials and you can easily move it aside when you're not working. The cloth prevents the beads from rolling around too much and provides a pleasant working surface. Or try using a shallow muffin tin or water-colour tray to keep different colours of beads separate.

PROBLEM: Not Enough Thread

Add thread using one of the following techniques if the thread breaks, if you have to cut the thread to remove an accidental knot or if the thread runs out. Many beading projects require a longer thread than you can comfortably work with; just use a comfortable length and add more thread when you need it.

For bead weaving techniques

1. Weave the old thread back through a few beads, tie an overhand knot around the thread between two beads, and pass the thread through a few more beads before cutting off the excess. (If you don't have enough thread left to do this, undo a bit of the beadwork to make room.) For extra security, you can knot it again and pass it through some more beads before trimming the excess.

2. Cut a new thread. Make it long enough to finish the work or as long as you can comfortably work with, whichever is shorter. Wax the thread if you are using unwaxed thread.

3. Start a short way back from the end of the beadwork. Leaving a short tail, weave the thread forward through a few beads, tie an overhand knot around the thread between two beads and weave forward to the point where you left off. (For extra security, knot in two places.) Cut off the tail of the new thread.

4. Use the new thread to continue beading as normal.

For loom work, trim the thread between two beads (rather than at the end of a row) so the tip doesn't show.

For stringing techniques

If you're stringing beads, the above method doesn't apply. Instead, go back a few beads and knot the new thread around the old thread. Pass the new thread forward through the last beads and knot the old thread around the new one. (If not enough old thread remains for a knot, take off a few beads to make room.) If you like, apply a tiny drop of adhesive to the knots before cutting off the thread tails.

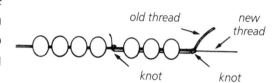

PROBLEM: Knots in the Thread

Knots are bound to occur when you use long pieces of thread; even waxed thread occasionally becomes knotted. In general, the thinner the thread, the more likely it is to tangle. Knots often develop when the tension of pulling it through a small bead hole twists the thread; if you keep pulling, it twists right into a knot. Knots form more readily on doubled thread because the two threads twist in opposite directions.

Prevention is the best solution. If you notice the thread twisting or coiling into loops, hold it straight with one hand and pull with the other. If you see a knot forming, stop what you're doing and untangle it while the knot is still loosely formed.

Here's what to do if a knot sneakily forms while you're looking the other way:

1. Try to loosen the knot. Slip a needle between the threads in the knot and pry them apart. If this doesn't work, go to the next step.

2. Pull the knot tight and continue beading. As long as the bead holes aren't too small, you can probably pull the knot through them. Eventually the knot will be hidden inside a bead. If the knot's too large to fit through the beads, go to the next step.

3. Cut the thread just before the knot. Place the needle on the remaining thread and carry on. If you are using doubled thread, thread both pieces through the eye of the needle. If the knot is near the beadwork, making the thread too short to continue beading, use the method for adding thread.

PROBLEM: Needle Won't Go Through a Bead

Occasionally the needle won't go through the bead one more time. Try the following solutions.

●Make sure the needle is not caught in a thread inside the bead.

●If the needle will go part of the way through, use pliers to carefully pull it the rest of the way through. Position the pliers at the place where the needle exits the bead, not down at the tip, or you may break the needle and have a new problem to contend with. (Use your judgement; if the pressure on the bead is too great, the bead may break.)

●Substitute a thinner needle. Keep a range of sizes on hand for this purpose.

●If the bead is close to the end of the beadwork, undo the beadwork and use a new bead with a larger hole.

●If you're weaving in a thread tail, choose a different route for the thread.

PROBLEM: Broken Bead

This solution is for off-loom and loom woven beadwork. Sometimes a bead breaks, if its hole is very small or several threads are already strung through it, when you try to pull another thread through. This is most likely to happen with seed or bugle beads. The best solution is prevention; see "Needle Won't Go Through a Bead" for different alternatives.

No matter how careful you are, accidents sometimes happen. If a bead breaks close to the end of the beadwork, of course, it's easy enough to undo the beadwork until you get to the broken bead and replace it with a new one.

Sometimes a bead breaks farther back in the work, when you're adding a new thread or when the work is already completed (for example, if you're adding a fringe or sewing together two pieces of beadwork). In this case, if you don't want to completely redo the beadwork, don't despair. There is another solution; it's similar to adding a new thread, but you also add a new bead.

1. Use a felt-tipped pen to mark the threads that went through the broken bead.

2. Prepare a new thread about 60 cm (2 feet) long.

3. Knot the new thread around the original thread between two beads, well back from the broken bead (for example, at least five rows back if you're doing loom woven beadwork). Leave about a 10 cm (4 inch) tail.

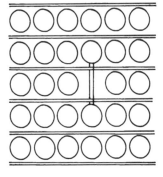

4. Following *exactly* the path of the original thread, weave the new thread through the beadwork until you reach the place where the bead broke. It's essential to follow the path exactly (under and over the warp threads, for example, if you're doing loom work), because soon you'll cut the original thread.

5. Add a new bead in the spot where the old bead broke.

6. Continue weaving the new thread through the beadwork, *exactly* following the original path, until you are well past the spot where the bead broke.

7. Knot the new thread around the original thread between two beads.

8. Cut *only* the marked threads at the spot where they went through the original bead, being very careful not to cut any other threads. Once you release the tension by cutting the old threads, the cut ends should retreat inside the neighbouring beads.

9. Weave both tails of the new thread through a few more beads, then cut them off.

This method is an invisible and secure way to replace broken beads.

PROBLEM: Broken Needle
Occasionally the needle will break as you work, usually when pulled through a tight hole. If you're using a single thread, just put a new needle on the thread. If you're using a doubled thread, cut the thread at the fold and thread both pieces through the eye of a new needle. You can also tie off the thread and continue beading with a new thread (following the instructions under "Not Enough Thread," but without weaving the old thread into the beadwork).

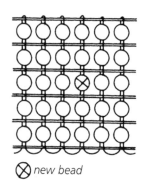

⊗ *new bead*

If you're having trouble inserting two pieces of thread through the eye of the needle, insert the first piece as normal, then pull the thread down and stretch it tightly against the bottom of the eye. This should allow plenty of room to insert the second thread. Another option is to weave one thread back into the beadwork and continue beading with a single thread.

Chapter Ten
Basic Knots

This chapter describes basic knots that are useful for anchoring threads in your beadwork.

DOUBLE HALF-HITCH
The double half-hitch is actually two *half-hitches* in a row. Use it to anchor one thread around another thread. It's also useful for knotting a single thread around a seed bead inside a calotte crimp.

GRANNY KNOT
The granny knot is composed of two *overhand knots*. You can tie a granny knot with a single thread or use it to knot two threads (or opposite ends of the same thread) together. Use it to knot two threads around a bead.

HALF-HITCH
The half-hitch will secure one thread to another. Use it for attaching the web cord to make dream catchers. It also works to fasten the warp threads of loom woven beadwork in the clean-edge finishing technique.

LARK'S HEAD KNOT
The lark's head knot, also called the *mounting knot*, anchors doubled threads. Use it for the *anchored netting* and *anchored right-angle weave* techniques (see Chapter 3, *Off-Loom Weaving*).

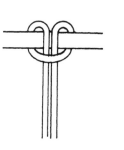

Basic Knots

MULTIPLE OVERHAND KNOT

The multiple overhand knot is also known as a *coil knot* and a *double knot*. It is similar to the *overhand knot*. Simply wrap the thread around the loop a few more times before pulling the knot tight. It's often used between pearls or beads on a strand (see Chapter 1, *Stringing*), when you want a larger knot than the overhand knot. The more times you wrap the thread around the loop, the larger the knot will be.

Note that the knot increases in size lengthwise; the multiple overhand knot creates a long, thin knot. If you want a wider knot, tie several overhand knots on top of each other.

OVERHAND KNOT

Also known as the *half knot*, the overhand knot is useful for knotting a thread around itself, around another thread or around a bead. It also works to knot the thread between beads, as described in Chapter 1, *Stringing*. Slip a needle in the loop before you tighten the knot and use the needle to slide the knot into position.

SLIDING KNOT

The sliding knot allows you to adjust your necklace or bracelet length; just slide the knots closer together or farther apart to achieve the right length. The sliding knot can replace a fastener on a snugly fitting piece of jewellery. Slide the knots together to put on a choker or bracelet, then draw the knots apart to tighten the fit. Use this knot with thick cords.

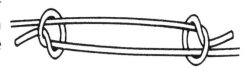

SLIP KNOT

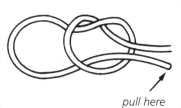

pull here

The slip knot is another variation of the *overhand knot*, in which one tail of thread is pulled back through the loop. The tail re-enters the loop on the same side of the loop-thread that it came from (in the diagram, it leaves and re-enters the loop *behind* the loop-thread, at the left side of the loop). This is the secret of the slip knot, which will temporarily hold beads in position on a thread. When you no longer need the knot, pull on the tail to undo the knot.

SQUARE KNOT

The square knot, also known as the *reef knot* or *flat knot*, is similar to but forms a stronger fastening than the *granny knot*. Use it to join the ends of a long strand of beads together, as described in Chapter 1, *Stringing*.

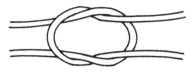

Chapter Eleven
Tools and Materials

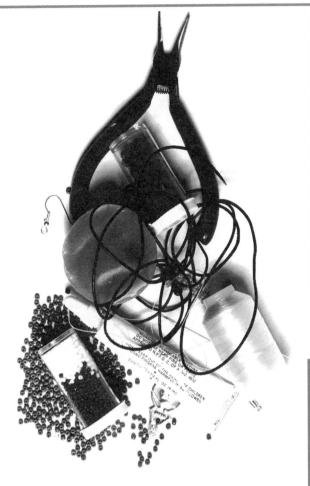

Basic materials that beginners need to get started or to do the projects in this book are included in this alphabetical list, and are denoted by the ✄ symbol. They fall into several main categories: adhesives, beads, beading needles, beading thread, beeswax, findings and pliers. See individual headings for more information. Note that alternative names are listed in parentheses after many of the terms in this chapter. The alternative names have a "see" reference to direct you to the main reference.

✄ **Adhesives.** Used to set knots and to attach **cabochons** to **ear posts**, **brooches** and other jewellery findings. Some professional beaders never use adhesive, but many beaders like using it for secure knots. Some prefer cement; others use clear nail polish or a colourless glue like Elmer's®, Super Tacky Glue® or Krazy Glue®. Mixed epoxy glue takes just five minutes to dry. Goop® is a rubber cement often sold in beading stores, but it's not very strong. (Caution: some glues

Tools and Materials

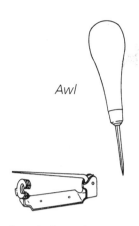

Awl

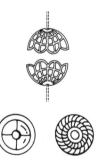

Bar pin brooch

Barrel clasp

Clean the threaded ends of the barrel clasp periodically so they close easily and securely. Otherwise they may come undone unexpectedly. Use a damp cloth or soapy water.

Bead caps

may discolour the finish on your beads; test glue on a few loose beads before applying it to your beadwork.) See also **clear nail polish** and **jeweller's cement**.

Adjustable ring. See **ring finding**.

Aron Alpha Jewellers' High Strength Instant Glue. See **jeweller's cement**.

Awl. A pointed tool used for making holes in leather or wood.

Bail or bale. See **triangle**.

Bar pin brooch (brooch back). A narrow metal bar with holes through which you fasten your beadwork; it has a pin on the back for attaching the brooch to clothing.

✿ *Barrel clasp.* This clasp has two parts that screw together. The beadwork is attached to a loop on each end of the clasp.

Barrette finding (hair clip). This easy-to-use finding consists of three detachable parts. The base has holes through which you fasten your beadwork. Barrette findings come in a range of sizes. (See diagram, page 102.)

✿ *Bead.* Beads are made of many natural and synthetic materials, and are available in a multitude of sizes, shapes and colours. Most have a hole drilled through or halfway through, but some have no hole at all. Explore your local bead or craft shop for beads from all over the world. See also **cabochon**, **micro bead**, **rondelle**, **spacer bead**, **stopper bead**, **trade bead**.

Bead board (bead stringing board). A wood or plastic tray with grooves, used in designing necklaces and bracelets. Most bead boards have rulers. Before stringing, lay a sequence of beads in a groove to see how they look together. As you work, use the narrow grooves to arrange beads by colour so you can scoop them quickly onto your needle.

Bead cap. A metal disk with a hole in the centre, curved to fit snugly against a bead. Bead caps are often filigreed or ornate, and come in various sizes. They protect a gemstone bead from the friction of rubbing against other surfaces. You can also use a bead cap instead of a **stopper bead** when you're making dangles, if the hole in a bead is too large and an **eye pin** or **head pin** would slip right through. Or use them for purely decorative reasons.

✿ *Bead loom.* Any commercial or self-made structure—usually of wood, metal or plastic—that will support the warp threads as you weave your beadwork. (See photo, page 69, and illustrations, page 72.)

Bead stop. See **stop spring**.

Bead stringing board. See **bead board**.

Bead tip. See **calotte crimp**.

Beading graph paper. Specialized graph paper that is used to plan beadwork designs for off-loom and loom weaving techniques. It is superior to regular graph paper because the beads are represented by rectangles or ovals rather than squares (a seed bead turned on its side is wider than it is long); some types are even scaled to suit specific seed bead sizes. Beading graph paper has been developed for loom work, *brick stitch, netting, peyote stitch* (both *one-* and *two-drop*), and *right-angle weave*. Peyote stitch graph paper can be turned 90° and used for the *brick stitch,* and vice versa; loom work graph paper can also be turned 90° and used for the *square stitch.* Some suppliers sell pads of beading graph paper, while others provide a reusable transparent template. If your bead store doesn't carry beading graph paper, ask the manager to special order it for you. See Chapter 8, *Planning and Design,* for information about using beading graph paper.

Beading needle. Needles are helpful in most beading projects, especially if you use a fine thread or beads with small holes. They are essential for working with **micro beads**. Beading needles come in different sizes and types. They're sized the same way as seed beads. You could use a size 10 needle with size 10 beads, though you might prefer a smaller needle, perhaps size 13, to allow more room for thread. Ordinary steel beading needles look like regular sewing needles but are much thinner. Their long, narrow holes (eyes) make them hard to thread. See also **glover needle**, **long needle**, **split wire needle**, **twisted wire needle**.

Beading thread. Any strand of synthetic or natural material used for threading or stringing beads. Countless materials are suitable for threading necklaces, bracelets, earrings and other beadwork. Your choice for a given piece of beadwork depends on the effect you wish to create and the type and size of beads you use.

Make sure that your thread, cord or wire will fit through the bead holes. Some techniques call for the thread to pass through the beads several times. In other cases beads can shift out of position if the cord is too thin. Also consider thread strength: check that the thread will support your beads' weight. (See Chapter 1, *Stringing,* for more information.)

Generally use a single thread unless directed otherwise. Many techniques call for a single thread if the thread must pass several times through small bead holes. To use a single thread, pull a few inches of thread through the needle (just enough so the needle won't fall off). To use a doubled thread, centre the needle on the thread to make two tails of equal length.

Clean beads with warm, soapy water. Test a few beads first, because water damages the finish on some types. Use a soft toothbrush, cloth or cotton swab to lift off grime, then rinse the beads with clear, lukewarm water. Dry the beads with a soft cloth (not paper towels, which can be abrasive). Never use solvents to clean beads. Don't immerse paper beads or porous beads such as coral, pearls and turquoise; just wipe them with a slightly damp cloth.

Beading needles

Keep a range of sizes of needles on hand so you can substitute a thinner needle to thread through small bead holes.

Tools and Materials

Tools and Materials

See also **elastic thread, fox-tail chain, invisible thread, lace, monofilament fishing line, nylon thread, precoiled steel bracelet and necklace wire, rattail, silk thread, tiger-tail, waxed nylon, wire.**

✿ ***Beeswax.*** Ordinary beeswax can be a beader's best friend. It can prevent long pieces of thread—required for most techniques—from knotting. If you're using unwaxed thread, run the thread twice over a lump of beeswax or an ordinary candle. Then pinch the thread between your thumb and forefinger, and pull it through with your other hand; this will distribute the wax evenly along the length of the thread and remove excess wax. Beeswax also strengthens the thread, prevents fraying, makes knots more secure and protects against moisture. The wax rubs off inside the beads, so remember to rewax periodically.

Bell cap

Bell cap (cord cap, end cap). A metal finding shaped like a bell, used to cap beads or knots. Use bell caps with a hole in the narrow end to neatly join multiple strands at the end of a piece of beadwork (as described in Chapter 1, *Stringing*). Use bell caps with a loop at the narrow end, and sometimes flexible claws at the wide end, for beads without a drilled hole. Set the bead in position with adhesive, then use the loop to attach the bead to your necklace, earring or other piece. Also see **cone.**

Bond 527 Multi-Purpose Cement. See **jeweller's cement.**

Brooch back. See **bar pin brooch.**

Brooch finding. Any finding used to make brooches. One type is a long pin with a hook-shaped loop at one end. After you put beads on the pin you bend it so the end catches in the loop (cut off excess wire, if any). Another type is shaped like a safety pin, with loops for attaching beadwork. See also **bar pin brooch, flat-backed brooch, hat pin, screened disk finding, stick pin.**

Brooch pin. See **brooch finding.**

Brooch finding

✿ ***Bugle bead.*** A tiny glass tube available in different sizes, colours and finishes. These beads are graded by their diameter and come in lengths ranging from 0.3 cm to 5 cm (1/8 inch to 2 inches). The longer the bugle beads, the more easily they break. Look for uniform size and smooth, unbroken ends when you buy bugle beads. When sorting through your bugle beads you may want to discard those with jagged edges. Another option is to use a fine metal **file** to make them smooth.

Butterfly. See **clutch, ear post.**

Cabochon. A flat-backed, rounded stone of glass, acrylic, or natural material. Use adhesive to attach cabochons to **ear posts** or other flat findings. (Chapter 2, *Earrings*, offers more information.)

✦ *Calotte crimp (bead tip).* Knot covers made of hinged cups with an attached loop. Some have a hole to thread through before you make a knot; others clamp over an already formed knot. The loop on the calotte crimp attaches to a clasp. Calotte crimps are sometimes erroneously called bead caps.

Cernit clay. See **polymer clay**.

Chain-nose pliers. See **needle-nose pliers**.

✦ *Chamois.* A soft, pliable leather. Imitation chamois is a cotton cloth finished to simulate this leather. Beaders use either as a backing for beadwork and appliquéd bead embroidery.

✦ *Clasp.* Any device or metal finding that attaches one end of your necklace or bracelet to the other. For bracelets, choose a type of clasp that you can fasten with one hand. See also **hook and chain fastener, jump ring, lobster clasp, screw clasp, snap clasp, snap hook, split ring, spring ring, tag**.

Claw clasp. See **lobster clasp**.

Clay. See **polymer clay**.

Clear fishing line. See **monofilament fishing line**.

✦ *Clear nail polish.* An alternative to **jeweller's cement** or other **adhesives**. Clear nail polish is invisible when dry and does not discolour beads. It works best with porous materials, for example, to set knots in thread. A disadvantage is that it is slow to dry. Make sure it dries completely before you move the beadwork, or the adhesive may not set properly.

Clip earring finding. A clip finding for unpierced ears or heavy earrings doesn't go through the ear, but clips onto the lower ear lobe. Some clips have a predecorated front and a loop for attaching beadwork. Other clips have a flat surface to glue stones onto or a woven mesh or screened disk to sew beads to. Bead shops sometimes sell small rubber pieces that you can glue to the back of clips to make them more comfortable.

Clutch (butterfly). A small metal or plastic piece that slides onto the end of an **ear post** to hold it in a pierced ear. (See ear post diagram, next page.)

Cone (cone cap, cone end cap). Similar to a **bell cap**, but shaped like a cone. Often filigreed, the cone has a hole at the narrow end. Use it to join multiple strands together.

Cord. See **lace**.

Cord cap. See **bell cap**.

Calotte crimp

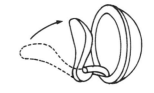
Clip earring finding

Cone

Tools and Materials

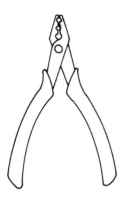

Crimping tool

Ear hoop

Ear post & clutch

✦ *Crimp.* Any metal finding used to secure the thread or cord at the ends of your necklace or bracelet. They provide a neat, professional finish. Crimps vary in size and type. Some attach the beadwork to the fastener so the thread is hidden. While not technically crimps, **bell caps**, **cones** and **end spacers** are used to secure multiple threads. See also **calotte crimp**, **end spring**, **French crimp**, **gimp**, **lace-end crimp**, **stop spring**.

Crimp bead. See **French crimp**.

Crimp bead pliers. See **crimping tool**.

Crimping tool. A tool specially designed to squeeze shut French crimps. It dents the crimp to separate the two threads, then bends the French crimp to form a round shape.

Cutters. See **wire snips**.

Dream catcher ear hoop. See **pinched hoop**.

E bead. See **pony bead**.

E6000. See **jeweller's cement**.

Ear clip. See **clip earring finding**.

Ear hoop. A thin wire hoop inserted through the hole in a pierced ear. Connect beadwork to the hoop with **jump rings** or string the hoop itself with beads. Some ear hoops have a shepherd's hook ear wire attached. Also see **pinched hoop**.

Ear post (stud). This wire post is inserted directly through a pierced ear and held in place with a **clutch (butterfly)**. You can attach your beadwork to the front of the post in many ways. Some findings have loops from which beads are suspended. Others have a cup and prong for securing half-drilled beads or a flat pad for fastening **cabochons**; use a strong adhesive to stick beads to these. Clean posts with rubbing alcohol or nail polish remover before glueing.

Ear wire. See **kidney ear wire**, **shepherd's hook ear wire**.

✦ *Earring finding.* Any metal material used to attach the beadwork part of the earring to the ear. See also **clip earring finding**, **clutch**, **ear hoop**, **ear post**, **kidney ear wire**, **screened disk finding**, **screw earring finding**, **shepherd's hook ear wire**.

Elastic thread. An alternative for large or medium-weight beads, elastic thread is handy when you don't want to use a fastener. Measure an appropriate length of elastic, string on your beads and tie the ends in a *square knot* (see Chapter 10, *Basic Knots*), hiding the join inside a bead.

Elmer's glue. See **adhesives**.

🌢 ***Embroidery hoop (tambour).*** Two rings, usually made of plastic or wood, that fit closely together to hold material taut and in position while you embroider with beads. Stretch the material tightly over the inner ring, then place the outer ring over both material and inner ring. Hoops are available in various sizes. See also **framing hoop**.

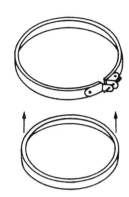

Embroidery hoop

End cap. See **bell cap**.

End coil. See **end spring**.

End spacer. A bar-shaped metal finding used to attach multiple strands to a clasp or single strand. It has several loops or holes on one side and a single loop or hole on the other side. See also **spacer bar**.

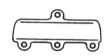
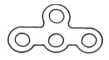

End spacers

End spring (end coil, leather crimp). A crimp made of coiled wire with a loop on one end, used to attach laces to a clasp. Double and triple end springs hold two and three laces respectively. Place the lace end in the end spring, position the pliers over the end of the coil and squeeze. The end of the coil bites into the lace. See also **lace-end crimp**.

Epoxy glue. See **adhesive**.

Eye pin. A flexible pin with a loop at one end. After you thread beads onto the pin, form a loop with the straight end and cut off the excess length. Eye pins are used to make dangles for earrings or necklaces, or to chain beads together instead of using thread. They come in several lengths and weights.

End spring

Fastener. See **clasp**.

🌢 ***File.*** Metal files are useful for smoothing the rough ends of **bugle beads**, **head pins**, **eye pins** or **stick pins**, and for roughing up **ear posts** before you glue on beads. Also see **needle file**.

Filler bead. See **spacer bead**.

Fimo clay. See **polymer clay**.

🌢 ***Finding.*** Any metal material used to make jewellery wearable, including all fasteners and anything that extends, connects or pins together your necklaces, earrings, bracelets, brooches, and so on. Most findings come in gold and silver tones, and range in style from simple to ornate. You can find detailed information on different findings and how to use them in the "Finishing Techniques" sections. See also **barrette finding**, **bead cap**, **brooch finding**, **clasp**, **crimp**, **earring finding**, **eye pin**, **head pin**, **ring finding**, **screened disk finding**, **triangle**.

Fishhook. See **shepherd's hook ear wire**.

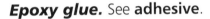

Eye pin

Tools and Materials

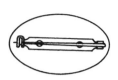

Flat-backed brooch

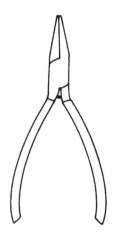

Flat-nose pliers

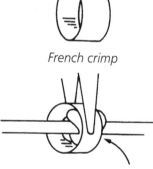

French crimp

Squeeze flat over knot

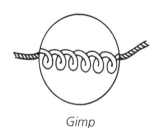

Gimp

Making a loop with gimp

Fishhook clasp. See **snap clasp**.

Flat-backed brooch. A brooch finding consisting of an oval metal plate with a pin on the back.

Flat-nose pliers. Pliers with flattened tips. They work well for squeezing shut **crimps** and bending wire, but they cannot form wire loops or rounded shapes.

Flat-pad ring. See **ring finding**.

Fox-tail chain. A heavy, braided silver-and-nickel chain, for use with heavy crystal or sharp metal beads. For an extra-secure fastening, you can solder the ends of the chain to the clasp. Otherwise, open the end links in the chain to attach **split rings**.

Framing hoop. An **embroidery hoop** with a built-in frame. Once you've finished embroidering the beadwork, it's ready to hang. Framing hoops are usually plastic in various colours including simulated wood grain. The circular hoops come in sizes from about 6.4 cm to 15 cm (2 1/2 inches to 6 inches) in diameter. The smallest oval hoops measure 5 cm by 7.6 cm (2 inches by 3 inches) and the largest are 12.7 cm by 17.8 cm (5 inches x 7 inches). If your bead store doesn't carry framing hoops, try a craft store.

French bullion. See **gimp**.

French crimp (crimp bead). A small metal ring that can be squeezed shut over knots made with nylon thread, silk thread or monofilament fishing line. It is also used to anchor **tiger-tail** and to hold beads in place on **stick pins**. Unlike a **calotte crimp**, a French crimp doesn't entirely conceal the thread, which is still visible where it loops through the clasp. If necessary you can use **gimp** to cover the thread.

French hook. See **shepherd's hook ear wire**.

French wire. See **shepherd's hook ear wire**.

Gimp (French bullion). A fine, flexible tubing made of coiled wire. It covers the part of the thread that loops through the clasp, both concealing the thread and preventing it from fraying. To use gimp, leave the needle on the thread once you finish the beadwork. Thread on 1.3 cm to 2 cm (1/2 inch to 3/4 inch) of gimp, then position the loop of your clasp over the gimp. Bend the bullion to form a loop, then weave the thread back into the beadwork. Gimp is also called French wire, but don't confuse it with ear wires of the same name. (See Chapter 1, *Stringing*, for information on using gimp.)

Glover needle. A special needle for sewing or embroidering leather. It has a very small eye and a three-sided point which allows the needle to glide easily through leather.

Glue. See **adhesive**.

Goop. See **adhesive**.

Graph paper. See **beading graph paper**.

Hair clip. See **barrette finding**.

Hat pin. A long, narrow pin traditionally used to hold a hat on the head; the pin pierces the hat and a thickness of hair, then emerges. Thread beads on them to make brooches.

Head pin. A wire pin with a flat head at one end. These pins come in various lengths and diameters, and are used to create dangles (by stringing beads on them and forming a loop in the straight end) for earrings and necklaces.

Heat-transfer pencil. A pencil used to transfer your bead embroidery design to fabric. Draw your design on **tracing paper** with the heat-transfer pencil. Place the paper on the material, drawn side down, and press with a heated iron.

Hook and chain fastener. A fastener that has two parts, a hook for one end of the beadwork and a chain for the other. This fastener is ideal when the fit of your necklace is important, because you can attach the hook to different chain links to adjust the length.

Hook and eye fastener. A common sewing fastener. Hooks and eyes are handy for connecting cloth fasteners that you make yourself and attach to wide pieces of beadwork.

Hoop. See **metal hoop**.

Hoop earring. See **ear hoop**.

Invisible thread. A transparent nylon thread that resembles a fine fishing line. It's less flexible than some threads, but useful for projects where the thread shouldn't show, such as woven seed bead earrings. As with monofilament fishing line, be careful not to kink the thread. If you have trouble finding it, try a fabric store.

Jeweller's cement. Adhesive that is made specifically for jewellery. Some beaders swear by **Aron Alpha Jewellers' High Strength Instant Glue**®. **E6000**® has a silicon base (like the caulking used on bathroom tiles) and is good for porous materials such as wood. **Bond 527 Multipurpose Cement**® is good for nonporous materials such as metal. It forms a strong bond, but takes about twenty-four hours to dry. As a general rule, the longer the drying time, the stronger the bond. Most adhesives bond better in warmer temperatures. See also **adhesive**.

Jump ring. A fine loop of wire with ends that press together. These small rings, used with clasps, attach one end of the beadwork to the

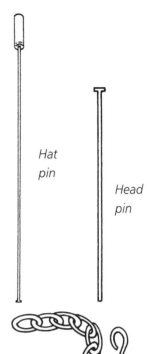

Hat pin

Head pin

Hook and chain fastener

Hook and eye fastener

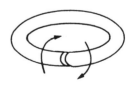

Jump ring

other. Always twist a jump ring sideways to open it. Pulling the ends apart in opposite directions will deform the ring and weaken the metal. After you've attached the jump ring to the beadwork, place a small drop of adhesive at the join to strengthen it.

Kidney ear wire

♦ *Kidney ear wire.* A thin wire loop that fits through a pierced ear; the top is rounded and the back hooks into the front. A kink in the front of the wire holds the beadwork; press the kink closed to keep it in place. Some kidney ear wires have a small loop instead of a kink.

Krazy glue. See **adhesive**.

♦ *Lace (cord, thong).* A material used to string beads with large holes. Laces are made of waxed cotton, leather, suede, deerskin and other materials, and come in many colours. Precut, one-metre (one-yard) lengths are handy for necklaces and chokers, but you can also have laces cut to any length you need. Their attractive finish makes them ideal for chokers, pendants and bracelets where the cord will show. See also **rattail**.

Lace-end crimp

♦ *Lace-end crimp.* A metal crimp that secures laces or cords to **clasps**. Squeeze the crimp shut over the tip of the lace, then attach the clasp or **jump ring** to the loop. You may wish to apply a drop of adhesive before closing the crimp.

Leather clasp. See **end spring**.

Leather cord. See **lace**.

Lobster clasp

Lobster clasp (claw clasp). This clasp works the same way as a **spring ring** but is shaped like a lobster claw instead of a ring. It's used with other findings (like **split rings** or **jump rings**); insert the ring in the opening that appears once you pull back the tab.

Long needle. A long beading needle of 7.6 cm to 10 cm (3 inches to 4 inches), used specifically for loom work. These needles range in thickness from size 10 down to size 16; the higher the number, the thinner the needle.

Long-nose pliers. See **needle-nose pliers**.

Loom. See **bead loom**.

Metal file. See **file**.

Metal hoop. Metal hoops, available in various sizes, are used to create beaded dream catchers.

Micro bead. A general term for small beads, ranging in size from 22° to 5° (1 mm to 0.7 cm, or 0.04 inch to 0.25 inch) in diameter. **Bugle beads**, **pony beads** and **seed beads** are included in this category. (See "Micro Bead Size Chart" on the next page.)

Mixed epoxy glue. See **adhesive**.

Monofilament fishing line (clear fishing line). An alternative for heavy beads, this transparent nylon line will weaken if it is bent. Its knots tend to come undone. Use **French crimps** to clamp the knots in place. You can also form a "knot" by melting the line into a ball at the end.

Needle. See **beading needle**.

Needle file. A rounded thin file that is useful for enlarging or clearing bead holes.

🖒 ***Needle-nose pliers (chain-nose pliers, long-nose pliers).*** All-purpose pliers, flattened on the inside where they press together but rounded on the outside. These pliers can close **crimps** and **jump rings**, and their rounded tips make it possible to form wire loops. Some come with built-in **wire snips**. If the jaws of the pliers are serrated, cover the tips with masking tape to avoid scratching or denting your wire. If you can only afford one pair of pliers, needle-nose pliers are your best bet. You can read about other pliers and get instructions on using them in Chapter 1, *Stringing*, and Chapter 2, *Earrings*.

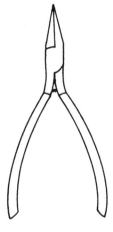

Needle-nose pliers

🖒 ***Nylon thread.*** Most frequently used with **seed beads** or other **micro beads**. It resembles ordinary sewing thread, but is much stronger, and comes in many colours and four weights (thicknesses). Precut lengths with attached needles are also available. Nylon thread works well for both weaving and stringing. One well-known brand is Nymo®. Some thread comes prewaxed to prevent knots and tangles; see **waxed nylon**.

Tools and Materials

MICRO BEAD SIZE CHART

1 mm	2 mm	3 mm	4 mm	5 mm	6 mm	3.2 mm	50.8 mm

● *The "°" (pronounced "ought") size system is a standardized grading system based on the diameter of the bead. The bigger the number, the smaller the bead.*

● *Once 22° was the smallest seed bead available; beads smaller than 18° are no longer made.*

● *10° and 11° are the commonest seed bead sizes and offer the largest variety of colours and finishes.*

● *Some bead stores now use a grading system based on the bead's diameter in millimetres. (Grade 2 = 2 mm, Grade 3 = 3 mm, etc.)*

● *Bugle beads are measured by their length and diameter. The diameter is sized using the same grading system as for seed beads; 10° and 11° are most common.*

Pinched hoop

Ring finding

Rondelles

Round-nose pliers

Nymo thread. See **nylon thread**.

Pinched hoop (dream catcher ear hoop). An ear hoop made especially for dream catcher earrings. The wire has grooves pinched into it at even intervals, for attaching the web cord. Also see **ear hoops**.

Pliers. See **flat-nose pliers**, **needle-nose pliers**, **round-nose pliers**.

Polymer clay. A plastic modelling substance used to make beads, available in many colours. Polymer clay yields results like regular clays, but it hardens at lower temperatures achievable in your kitchen oven. Popular brands include Cernit®, Fimo® and Sculpey®.

🖊 ***Pony bead (E bead).*** A small glass bead larger than about 0.3 cm (0.12 inch) in diameter; the largest E beads measure about 0.6 cm (0.25 inch) in diameter. Pony beads are in the **micro bead** category but are not considered **seed beads**. They can be used with the same techniques as seed beads.

Post. See **ear post**.

Precoiled steel bracelet and necklace wire. This strong wire can form necklaces and bracelets that coil around the neck or wrist several times; no fastener is necessary. Simply string on your beads and use pliers to form a loop at each end so the beads don't fall off.

Prewaxed thread. See **waxed nylon**.

Rattail (satin cord). A thick rayon-wrapped cord, well suited for stringing large beads. Rattail comes in three weights and many colours. Its beautiful satiny finish makes it ideal for pieces of beadwork where you want parts of the cord to show. Also see **lace**.

Ring finding (flat-pad ring). A plain ring with a flat pad at the front, often with a split at the back of the band for adjusting the size. See also **screened disk finding**.

Rocaille. See **seed bead**.

Rondelle. A decorative metal disk used as a **spacer bead**. The outer edge is set with rhinestones or crystals. Rondelles are often used in pearl necklaces.

🖊 ***Round-nose pliers.*** Pliers that have completely round tips. They are essential for forming wire into loops and scrolls when creating jewellery fasteners.

Ruler. See **tape measure**.

Safety clasp. See **snap clasp**.

Safety glasses. Use these to protect your eyes when working with wire. You can purchase them cheaply at most hardware stores.

Satin cord. See **rattail**.

🪝 *Scissors.* An essential beading tool! Scissors with narrow tips are best; they allow you to cut thread close to the beadwork.

Screened disk finding. A jewellery finding that has two parts: a curved metal disk with holes or a fine wire mesh, and a back piece attached to a brooch pin, earring finding or ring. Some types have claws on the disk, while others have claws on the backing. After you anchor beads to the disk by threading through the holes, clip the back part on and bend the claws to hold the disk in place.

Screened disk findings

Screw clasp. Any metal clasp that has two parts that screw together. Usually each end of the clasp will have a loop to which you attach beadwork. These clasps come in a multitude of shapes and sizes. See also **barrel clasp**, **torpedo clasp**.

Screw earring finding

Screw earring finding. Findings that screw at the back of the ear lobe for unpierced ears or heavy earrings. They come in various types; some have loops for hanging beads, others have a flat piece for setting a stone with adhesive.

Sculpey clay. See **polymer clay**.

🪝 *Seed bead (rocaille).* A tiny round bead made of glass or metal. Seed beads are used in many of the techniques in this book. They are graded in size, ranging from size 22° to 10° (0.1 cm to 0.3 cm, or 0.04 inch to 0.12 inch) in diameter. The smaller beads are no longer manufactured and are harder to find. Seed beads come in many colours and various finishes. They are sold in vials or packets, or are strung on groups of threads; this last is called a hank of beads.

There are different qualities of seed beads. When you buy them, look for consistent shapes and hole sizes. Modern Japanese beads are among the most consistent. Lower quality beads have irregularities and their holes are often only partially formed.

Sewing snap. A common sewing fastener. Snaps are handy for connecting cloth fasteners that you make yourself and attach to wide pieces of beadwork.

Shepherd's hook ear wire (Fishhook, French hook, French wire). A thin wire hook for pierced ears, with loops for suspending beadwork.

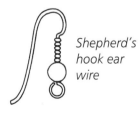

Shepherd's hook ear wire

🪝 *Silk thread.* This thread is ideal for semiprecious stones and heavier beads with finely drilled holes. Silk thread is strong and doesn't stretch much, but it does tend to fray. It's available in various colours and weights (white silk comes in eleven different weights), but is more expensive than regular nylon thread. It's also more prone to decay than nylon thread.

Snap. See **sewing snap**.

Snap clasp (fishhook clasp, safety clasp). A clasp consisting of

Snap clasp

Tools and Materials

Snap hook

Spacer bar

Split ring

Spring ring

Stop spring

two pieces that snap or hook together. The sections come apart only if you press the tab to release the catch. Loops at either end are for connecting your beadwork; some styles have several loops for fastening multistrand beadwork. Snap clasps come in many sizes and styles, some engraved or filigreed.

Snap hook. A clasp made of a thin strip of metal, with the two ends overlapping. Slip a **jump ring**, **split ring** or **tag** between the overlapping ends.

Spacer bar. A bar-shaped finding made of metal or leather, with several holes for keeping multiple strands separate. Spacer bars can be used at the ends of beadwork or used throughout and incorporated into the design. Pass one or more strands through each hole to keep them in position. Also see **end spacer**.

Spacer bead. A bead used to separate or accent other beads.

Split ring. A fine metal ring similar to a **jump ring**, but with overlapping ends. These small rings work together with clasps to attach one end of the beadwork to the other.

Split wire needle. Two parallel flexible wires joined at each end, forming a needle that's almost all eye. This feature makes it easier to thread than a regular beading needle.

Spring ring. A metal clasp used with **jump rings**, **split rings** or **tags**. When you pull back the tab, the spring ring opens; insert your jump ring, split ring or tag. The spring ring usually has a loop to which you attach one end of the beadwork.

Stackable fishing tackle containers. Transparent containers that screw into each other, with a lid at the top of the stack. They're ideal for storing small beads.

Steel beading needle. See **beading needle**.

Stick pin. A long, thin metal pin, easily threaded with beads. Hold beads in place with adhesive or a **French crimp**. The finished pin can decorate a hat or piece of clothing.

Stop spring (bead stop). A crimp made of coiled wire, used to hold beads in position on laces. Thread the stop spring into position on the lace, then squeeze the ends of the coil with pliers so they bite into the lace. See also **French crimp**.

Stopper bead. A small bead used to prevent a bead with a large hole from slipping off an **eye pin** or **head pin**.

Stud. See **ear post**.

Super Tacky Glue. See **adhesive**.

Tag. A flat piece of metal with a small hole at one end and a large hole at the other, used with a clasp to fasten a necklace or bracelet. Attach the beadwork to the small hole and insert the clasp (such as a **spring ring**) through the large hole.

Tag

🖉 **Tailor's chalk.** Chalk used to transfer your bead embroidery design to the fabric. Because chalk rubs off easily, it is only a temporary marker.

Tambour. See **embroidery hoop**.

🖉 **Tape measure.** Used to measure thread and work in progress. You can use a ruler, but a tape measure is preferable because it's longer and flexible. It's hard to measure your neck circumference with a ruler!

Thong. See **lace**.

Thread. See **beading thread**.

🖉 **Threader.** A tool designed to help you thread your needle. Your package of needles may include a threader, but use it with care. Since beading needles are much thinner than ordinary sewing needles, a threader can break the delicate metal surrounding the needle's eye.

Threader

Tiger-tail. A nylon-coated stainless steel wire used for heavy, metal or sharp beads. It is available in three weights. Although tiger-tail will not fray, it's unsuitable for light beads because it's too stiff. Leave a bit of excess wire when you attach the fasteners to allow the beads more freedom of movement so they hang naturally.

🖉 **Tool kit.** You need three tools to start your personal tool kit: a good pair of sharp **scissors**, a **tape measure** or ruler to measure your thread and work in progress, and a pair of **needle-nose pliers.** These are handy when you apply your finishing technique; pliers with built-in wire snips are ideal.

Tools. See **awl**, **crimping tool**, **file**, **pliers**, **scissors**, **wire snips**.

Torpedo clasp. A cylindrical clasp with two parts that screw together. Attach the **beading thread** or **crimp** to the loop on each part of the clasp.

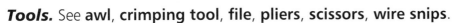

Torpedo clasp

🖉 **Tracing paper (transfer paper).** Similar to tissue paper—thin and transparent. Use it to transfer an embroidery design to fabric.

🖉 **Trade bead.** Beads that European explorers used for trade in Africa and North America beginning in the sixteenth century. They were also used for trade from China to North America. These larger glass beads are now antiques, but people also use this term for any beads that are traded or bartered. The "trade" beads manufactured today—from clay, glass or plastic—are popular, affordable imitations.

Tools and Materials

Triangle

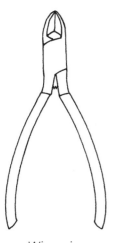

*Twisted wire
needle*

Wire snips

Transfer paper. See **tracing paper**.

Triangle (bail or bale). A triangular metal finding with two straight prongs that you insert into a bead to hold it securely. Use the top part of the triangle as you would a loop to attach the bead to an earring finding or necklace.

Twisted wire needle. An extremely flexible needle with a large, collapsible eye. It can be used for both stringing and off-loom weaving. A drawback is that this needle type quickly becomes bent out of shape.

Wax. See **beeswax**.

Waxed nylon (prewaxed thread). A thread that comes pre-waxed to prevent knots and tangles. You can buy it in three weights and a variety of colours.

Wire. A material for stringing large, heavy or sharp beads. You can also use it to create jewellery findings such as **eye pins** and **triangles**. Wire comes in different sizes (gauges) and even different colours. A 28-gauge wire is thin and threadlike; a 10-gauge wire is thick and heavy. Use 22- to 28-gauge wire for stringing and 18- to 22-gauge wire for making jewellery findings. Wire also comes in different shapes: round, half-round, square, triangle and twist. Round wire is easiest to find and will suit most of your jewellery-making needs.

Wire snips (cutters). A special tool designed for cutting wire. Some pliers have built-in wire cutters.

Bibliography

Barth, Georg J. *Native American Beadwork: Traditional Beading Techniques for the Modern-Day Beadworker.* Stevens Point, Wisconsin: R. Schneider Publisher, 1993.

Beck, Horace C. *Classification and Nomenclature of Beads and Pendants.* York, Pennsylvania: Liberty Cap Books, 1973. (Originally published in *Archaeologia*, Volume LXXVII, 1928.)

Benson, Ann. *Beadweaving: New Needle Techniques & Original Designs.* New York: A Sterling Chapelle Book, Sterling Publishing Co. Inc., 1993.

Coles, Janet and Robert Budwig. *The Book of Beads: A Practical and Inspirational Guide to Beads and Jewelry Making.* New York: Simon and Schuster. London: Dorling Kindersley Limited, 1990.

Dubin, Lois Sherr. *The History of Beads: From 30,000 B.C. to the Present.* New York: Harry N. Abrams, Inc., 1987.

Duncan, Kate C. *Northern Athapaskan Art: A Beadwork Tradition.* Vancouver, British Columbia: Douglas & McIntyre Ltd., 1989.

Erikson, Joan Mowat. *The Universal Bead.* New York: W.W. Norton & Company Inc., 1969.

Giltsoff, Natalie. *Fashion Bead Embroidery.* London: B.T. Batsford Limited. Newton, Massachusetts: Charles T. Branford Company, 1971.

Hunt, W. Ben and J. F. Burshears. *American Indian Beadwork.* 1951. New York: Collier Books, Macmillan Publishing Co., Inc., 1971.

Kidd, Alexandra. *Beautiful Beads: How to Create Beautiful Original Gifts & Jewelry for Every Occasion.* Radnor, Pennsylvania: A Quarto Book, Chilton Book Co., 1994.

La Croix, Grethe. *Beads Plus Macramé: Applying Knotting Techniques to Beadcraft.* Little Craft Book Series. New York: Sterling Publishing Co. Inc. Don Mills, Ontario: Saunders of Toronto, Ltd. London: Ward Lock, Ltd., 1971. (Translated by Eric Greweldinger, adapted by Jane Lassner, original title *Draad en Kralen.* De Bilt, Netherlands: Cantecleer De Bilt, 1969.)

Lightbody, Donna M. *Let's Knot: A Macramé Book.* New York: Lothrop, Lee and Shepard Co., 1972.

Luters, Ginger. "Clay Play," *Bead & Button.* Feb. 1994: 16–18.

McNeill, Suzanne. *Beaded Dream Catchers.* Fort Worth, Texas: Design Originals, 1994.

McNeill, Suzanne. *Thong Beading.* Fort Worth, Texas: Design Originals, 1994.

Monture, Joel. *The Complete Guide to Traditional Native American Beadwork: A Definitive Study of Authentic Tools, Materials, Techniques and Styles.* New York: Collier Books, Macmillan Publishing Company, 1993.

Moss, Kathlyn and Alice Scherer. *The New Beadwork.* New York: Harry N. Abrams, Inc., 1992.

Nathanson, Virginia. *The Pearl and Bead Boutique Book.* Great Neck, New York: Hearthside Press Inc. Publishers, 1972.

Orchard, William C. *Beads and Beadwork of the American Indians.* New York: Museum of American Indians, Heye Foundation, 1975.

Poris, Ruth F. *Advanced Beadwork.* Tampa, Florida: Golden Hands Press, 1989.

Poris, Ruth F. *Step-by-Step Bead Stringing: A Complete Illustrated Professional Approach.* Tampa, Florida: Golden Hands Press, 1984.

Reid, Laura. *Adventures in Creating Earrings.* Liberty, Utah: Eagle's View Publishing, 1990.

Roche, Nan. *The New Clay: Techniques and Approaches to Jewelry Making.* Rockville, Maryland: Flower Valley Press, 1991.

Scholz-Peters, Ruth. *Indian Bead Stringing and Weaving.* New York: Sterling Publishing Co. Inc., 1975. (Translated by Maxine Hobson. Originally published in Germany as *Perlen Gewebt und Gefädelt,* 1974.)

Seyd, Mary. *Introducing Beads.* London: B.T. Batsford Limited. New York: Watson-Guptill Publications, 1973.

Sherwood, Jane. *Beaded Barrettes and Bracelets.* Lakeside, California: Sherwood Designs, 1991.

Sherwood, Jane. *Beaded Necklaces.* Lakeside, California: Sherwood Designs, 1989.

Sherwood, Jane. *Glamour Earrings for Beginners.* Lakeside, California: Sherwood Designs, 1990.

White, Mary. *How to Do Beadwork.* 1904. New York: Dover Publications Inc., 1972.

Wildschut, William and John C. Ewers. *Crow Indian Beadwork: A Descriptive and Historical Study.* 1959. Liberty, Utah: Eagle's View Publishing, 1985.

Woodsmall, Annabel Whitney. *Contemporary Appliqued Beadwork: Threads in Action; Monograph II.* Freeland, Washington: HTH Publishers, 1979.

Wynne-Evans, Sigrid. "Beaded Crystal Bottles," *Jewelry Crafts.* Apr. 1995: 26–30.

Zamot, Jean A. *The Art of Bead and Pearl Stringing: A Workbook and Reference Manual.* Whittier, California: Gems, Etc., 1985.

Acknowledgements

The evolution of this book taught me two important things: anything is possible if I take it one small step at a time, and I have more than my share of wonderfully supportive people in my life.

I'd first like to thank Stephen Ogden of the Print Futures program at Douglas College, who inspired me to write this book. Once I took the plunge and began writing, many people appeared at just the right moment. Kim Rempel, Vera Markovich, Bev Lytton and Wilf Higgins gave me encouragement and much more. David Cameron, Sean Adkins and Guy Robertson all helped in the early stages. I am indebted to my colleagues at Computer Associates for their understanding, and to Heather Sommerville for teaching me to write better. Anne and Helen Werry of Milestone Publications gave me key advice on publishing. Katherine Dudgeon aided by always seeing (and telling me) the truth.

I am grateful to line editor Susan Mayse for her delicate touch and I'll owe an eternal debt of gratitude to project editor Marisa Alps for a hundred things.

Many excellent professional beaders shared their knowledge to make this book the best it could be. Debbie Rice of Crafty Cat Art, Bead and Gift Shop and Karen and Harley Glesby of the Silver Moon Trading Co. Ltd. gave generously of their time and work. Jacqui Bellefontaine advised in many areas and Angela Swedberg contributed her renowned expertise to the section on embroidery. I am thankful to all the beaders who shared their work with me and regret not all of it could be included.

It was a particular honour to have the unsparing attention of one of North America's finest beading scholars, Alice Scherer, co-author of *The New Beadwork* and Director of the Center for the Study of Beadwork.

I extend my heartfelt gratitude to Graeme Teixeira, former president of Beadworks / Worldbeads. His expert advice, kindness and faith in the book gave me the courage to continue.

Index

Note: Page numbers followed by "wt" refer to a Working Tip in the margin.

Index

Index

Karen Rempel was born in Vancouver, British Columbia, and has lived in the Vancouver area her entire life. She graduated from Simon Fraser University and currently works as a self-employed technical writer.

She has published fiction, poetry, feature articles and reviews in publications including *The Vancouver Sun, Herspectives, Discorder* and *BC Woman Magazine. Complete Beading for Beginners* is her first book.

Karen Rempel discovered beading when she was ten years old. She began borrowing beading books from the library, and soon was spending her entire allowance on beads. Although she has experimented with many different types of beads, she prefers to work with seed beads, and has collected over a hundred different colours. She explains, "I like seed beads because I don't have the talent to express colour by painting, but somehow with beads I can capture the pictures I see in my mind." She says that while she may forget about beadwork when her life gets too busy, she is always drawn back to it: "For me, beading is a spiritual activity that allows me to express my creativity, work through issues in my life, and perhaps even tap into the collective unconscious—that great store of human memories and knowledge that is even older than beads."